Implementing Lean Six Sigma in 30 Days

Implement the world's most powerful improvement
methodology in 30 days

Gopal Ranjan

Tanmay Vora

Impackt Publishing
We Mean Business

Implementing Lean Six Sigma in 30 Days

First published: October 2014

Production reference: 1251014

Published by Impackt Publishing Ltd.
Livery Place
35 Livery Street
Birmingham B3 2PB, UK.

ISBN 978-1-78300-034-0

www.impacktpub.com

Cover image by Jarek Blaminsky (milak6@wp.pl)

Credits

Authors
Gopal Ranjan
Tanmay Vora

Reviewers
Professor V. K. Garg
Alaeddin Hallak
Sarabjeet S. Kochar
Sidhartha Mukherjee

Acquisition Editor
Richard Gall

Proofreaders
Simran Bhogal
Ameesha Green
Paul Hindle

Copy Editors
Tanvi Bhatt
Maria Gould
Paul Hindle
Alfida Paiva
Faisal Siddiqui

Project Coordinator
Priyanka Goel

Production Coordinator
Melwyn D'sa

Cover Work
Melwyn D'sa

About the Authors

Gopal Ranjan has extensive experience in developing breakthrough improvements and quality management systems. He is a certified Six Sigma Master Black Belt with more than 16 years of experience in the design and deployment of Lean Six Sigma methodology across different organizations. He is also a certified Balanced Scorecard Practitioner. He is also the Lead Auditor on ISO 9001 and ISO 27001 standards. He holds a BTech degree from India's prestigious Indian Institute of Technology, BHU, Varanasi, as well as a Master's degree in Business Administration in Finance. He is also a practicing NLP practitioner and holds a Master's degree in Psychotherapy and Counseling. He regularly writes articles and columns on varied subjects including management, science, psychology, and philosophy for newspapers and magazines. Currently, he heads the Quality function of one of India's foremost IT services companies, Datamatics Global Services Ltd. He can be reached at gopalranjan_2000@ yahoo.com.

This book has benefited from the support of a large number of people. I apologize for not listing them all. A few people played a major role in making this book happen. First of all, I would like to thank my parents who always believed in me and encouraged me to explore new horizons and kept the tap of curiosity open. My wife, Anupam, who always stood by me and provided critical feedback about the content and the structure of the book. My elder brother, Rajeev, who always goaded me to pen down a book. My editor, Richard Gall, who went through the manuscript patiently many times and provided valuable assistance throughout the writing process. Our coordinator, Priyanka Goel, who ensured that everything was in order and the project was on time. Last but not least, my young daughters, Kashvi and Advika, for providing the pep and energy to bring the book to its logical conclusion.

Tanmay Vora is a quality professional who has 15 years of diverse IT experience leading corporate quality programs, growing software testing teams, providing process consulting, and driving improvement initiatives. He currently leads a corporate quality program at CIGNEX Datamatics where he spearheaded certification initiatives such as CMMI Level 3 and ISO 27001 (Information Security).

At QAspire Blog, which he founded in 2006, Tanmay combines his passion for writing with his deep interest in excellence, people, leadership, and human aspects of building a culture of excellence. He recently wrote his first book titled *#QUALITYtweet – 140 bite sized ideas to deliver quality in every project*, THINKaha, and he regularly contributes his writing to various blogs, magazines, and books. In 2012 and 2013, he was rated as one of the *Top 5 Indian HR Influencers on Social Media* by the Society of Human Resources Management (SHRM India).

Tanmay tweets as `@tnvora` and can be contacted at `tanmay.vora@gmail.com`.

This book was not possible without the subject matter expertise of my co-author Gopal Ranjan. I totally appreciate his constant support and guidance.

My family has been a constant source of inspiration for me and I am grateful for the love and encouragement they provide in all my endeavors, including this book.

Thanks also to my editor, Richard Gall, for reviewing the manuscript, and the members of the Packt Publishing team who collaborated with us to make this book happen.

About the Reviewers

Professor V. K. Garg carries with him over 35 years of experience in the fields of information technology, management consulting, and academics. He has been on the boards of various companies for over 10 years and has worked with well-known organizations such as A F Ferguson, Larson and Turbo, Zenith Computers, NITIE, Lupin Laboratories, Rolta, Datamatics, and others. He is an acknowledged authority in the various areas related to project management. He has also been associated with various World Bank sponsored projects as an expert.

As a corporate trainer and consultant, he is associated with many leading IT organizations and institutions. He is the brain behind two of the training programs that have been highly appreciated by various State Electricity boards and Public Welfare departments around Project Identification Formulation and Appraisal (PIFA) and Project Implementation Monitoring and Control (PIME) with the help of World Bank. His training programs are well recognized, widely accepted, and attended by senior and middle management personnel from diverse industries and government agencies. He is a much sought after trainer, and his diverse disciplinary experience equips him with a wide perspective and deep insights into the challenges and issues of the business world.

Professor Garg is also a certified Six Sigma Master Black Belt and has been the guiding force behind over 200 Six Sigma and Lean Six Sigma projects in various organizations for more than 10 years.

He is the author of two best-selling books—*Enterprise Resource Planning*, and *Workbook on System Analysis & Design*, both published by Prentice-Hall of India Publications. Both these books have run into multiple editions. He also has to his credit numerous articles and research papers that have been published in leading journals and conference proceedings.

Prof. Garg is a gold medalist in Bachelor of Engineering and an MTech from the prestigious Indian Institute of Technology (IIT), Delhi.

Alaeddin Hallak is a senior business analyst and a Six Sigma Green Belt at HP Enterprise Services. He currently leads the business analysis team at SADAD Payment System, Saudi Arabia's national payment gateway that handles over 90 percent of the Kingdom's payment transactions. Previously, he was the lead BPM specialist for several Saudi government institutions including the General Authority of Civil Aviation, Jeddah Municipality, and Royal Commission for Jubail and Yanbu.

A graduate of Computer Science from the Jordan University of Science and Technology, Alaeddin holds several industry qualifications in business analysis and IT. He is a Certified Business Analysis Professional (CBAP), Certified Six Sigma Green Belt, TOGAF 9 Certified, and a Certified Usability Analyst. His diverse training and over 9 years of experience in and outside IT gives him a unique perspective on approaching business problems from different angles and building solutions that facilitate optimum change for the business.

Sarabjeet S. Kochar is a Mechanical Engineering graduate from Thapar University with over 13 years of experience in the field of quality. He has rich experience of deploying quality systems and improvement methodologies, such as Six Sigma and Lean, in multiple industries and environments. His experience also includes the set up and governance of various improvement methodologies. Most recently, Sarabjeet has been a part of one of the largest financial services companies in the world, deploying Six Sigma at their processing centers and customer-facing businesses. He has been leading a team of Black Belts providing high-impact benefits to the business in terms of efficiency, customer experience, risk mitigation, and loss mitigation. He has also been program managing various multi-shore projects.

Sarabjeet has been involved in the development and delivery of Six Sigma training curriculums and materials as part of his roles involving Six Sigma deployment.

He has also been involved in multiple community service / volunteering efforts supporting organizations that give back to the community.

Sidhartha Mukherjee, or Sid, began studying and applying Six Sigma during his MBA days at Symbiosis (2006-08). As a part of the Operations Management curriculum, he had the opportunity to attend an introductory GB-level training in Six Sigma, conducted by KPMG. The certification process required working on an industrial Six Sigma project, giving him a chance to augment his classroom learning with first-hand implementation. The challenges of real-world process improvement including statistical data analysis, value streams, and change management proved too exciting, and Sid decided to make it a post-MBA career choice. He started his process improvement career with WNS Global Services (formerly a captive unit of British Airways) in Pune. Since then, he has worked in Process Improvement roles with Genpact (formerly GE Capital) and HSBC Technology and Services (as a Process Reengineering Consultant), in addition to freelance projects. Today, he works as a Process and Quality Consultant with Cognizant Business Consulting and is based in Pune, India.

In his career spanning 8.5 years so far (up to the time of publication), Sid has had the opportunity to work on process efficiency and cost reduction, process reengineering, and variation and NVA reduction across a wide variety of domains including finance and accounting services, banking and financial services, and IT application and maintenance services (his current field of engagement).

Sidhartha is a BE and MBA by education—he received his Bachelor's degree in Electrical Engineering from the Visvesvaraya Technological University (VTU) in 2003, and an MBA in Operations Management in 2008 from the Symbiosis Institute of Operations Management (Symbiosis International University) in India. He is also a certified Master Black Belt (Indian Statistical Institute), as well as being a certified BB from ASQ and SSMI.

In addition to projects, Sid is passionate about delivering performance improvement training using Lean and Six Sigma methods, and is a passionate people-person who believes in driving sustainable, long-term change through a combination of metrics, reengineering, and motivation. A firm believer in personal and professional Kaizen, Sid's vision for himself is to contribute to organizations by offering a value-based skillset of performance, change, and project management.

Beyond work, Sid can be found spending time with family and friends, travelling to offbeat locations, volunteering at blood-donation camps, and listening to music, especially when navigating the treacherous and variation-afflicted terrain of the Calcutta area traffic.

I would like to thank the following people.

To my father, Deb Kumar Mukherjee, for exemplifying the true meaning of "selfless work and service" in all aspects of life. If I can be half the man that you've been, I'll consider my life to have been a success.

To my mother, Rekha Mukherjee, for teaching me to be a kind and compassionate human being, to be humble in success and gracious in all occasions.

To my sister, Paromita Bhattacharya, for teaching me the values of righteousness and for being a constant source of support and encouragement. Sis, looks like both of us made it in our respective fields, with a lot of ground still left to cover!

To my brother-in-law, Dr. Subhamoy Bhattacharya, thanks for being more than a brother, and taking care of my dear sister. Also, to all of you for never losing faith in me.

Lastly, to my dear nephew, Ishan Bhattacharya (Tito), you're the greatest thing that's happened to us, the light of our lives, and we can't wait to see you grow up!

Contents

Preface

Lean Six Sigma is a process-improvement program that synergizes the power of two of the most successful and widely deployed improvement programs—Lean and Six Sigma. This combined program distils the strengths of the two: Lean with its focus on eliminating waste and making processes faster, and Six Sigma with its focus on reducing variation and defects. The results are a truly potent combination, effectively addressing the bottom line of an organization.

There are many excellent books on Lean Six Sigma. However, the majority of these books primarily deal with the theory behind the methodologies and tools involved, with almost negligible thrust on the practical implementation and challenges involved. A need has been constantly felt for a book that can serve as a bridge between theory and practice. This book, *Implementing Lean Six Sigma in 30 Days*, serves exactly this purpose.

This is a *practical guide* that should be viewed as a companion for the implementation of Lean Six Sigma. It arms you with the key concepts and explains the steps involved in a successful implementation of the methodology in an easy-to-understand and reader-friendly format. This book is a *handy reference guide* that covers all that one needs to know about Lean Six Sigma for *most common applications*. It aims to provide you with a "narrative" that can be used by a practitioner at all levels—beginner to advanced levels. An easy-to-understand and practical day-wise format makes the implementation process less challenging and more effective.

Each of the chapters that follow is supported by an ongoing case study to help you bridge the gap between the theory and execution. You will also find a quiz at the end of each chapter, which should help you consolidate what you have learned.

What this book covers

Chapter 1, *What is Lean Six Sigma?*, deals with the key concepts and principles behind both Lean and Six Sigma to give you a solid theoretical basis from which you can begin your implementation.

Chapter 2, *Planning the Implementation*, takes you through the key steps involved in the implementation, and divides each step into a day-by-day format so that you can visualize the process and gain a clear understanding of how it should unfold.

Chapter 3, *Define (Days 9-11)*, explores the process of identifying and understanding the issues that the implementation of Lean Six Sigma will attempt to resolve. This is critical; having a clear understanding and a thorough definition of a problem is essential to ensuring that the implementation provides successful results.

Chapter 4, *Measure (Day 12-17)*, describes the tools and metrics that are vital to gaining a greater understanding of the issues you may have recognized at the "Define" stage. Once you have a handle on the figures and statistics that describe your current situation, you should be able to recognize precisely where you want to be and how you are going to get there.

Chapter 5, *Analyze (Day 14-19)*, outlines the tools and techniques to uncover the causes of the problems you have both defined and measured. This will help you as you begin your initiative for improvement.

Chapter 6, *Improve (Days 20-25)*, builds on your findings from the previous chapter, guiding you through the initial actions that need to be taken as part of the Lean Six Sigma implementation.

Chapter 7, *Control (Days 26-30)*, aims to show you how to sustain the improvements that you have made to ensure that the Lean Six Sigma implementation produces lasting results.

Chapter 8, *Best Practices and Pitfalls*, shares some of the most common and effective best practices used by successful companies as well as pitfalls that need to be avoided during the implementation of Lean Six Sigma.

Who this book is for

Written for the forward thinking and ambitious, this book will give you the foundational knowledge on how to improve your organization. With practical and applicable advice, you will discover how to control quality and improve efficiency, giving you the confidence to drive your company to success.

Conventions

In this book, you will find a number of styles of text that distinguish between different kinds of information. Here are some examples of these styles and an explanation of their meaning.

New terms and **important words** are shown in bold like this: "Once there is clarity and commitment from the top management and goals and objectives are put in place, the second step, **Enable**, involves the selection and training of key people who will actually drive the initiative."

Make a note

Warnings or important notes appear in a box like this.

Tip

Tips and tricks appear like this.

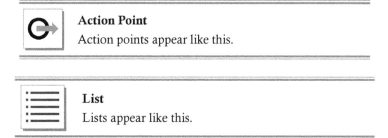

Action Point

Action points appear like this.

List

Lists appear like this.

Reader feedback

Feedback from our readers is always welcome. Let us know what you think about this book—what you liked or may have disliked. Reader feedback is important for us to develop titles that you really get the most out of.

To send us general feedback, simply send an e-mail to feedback@impacktpub.com, and mention the book title via the subject of your message.

Piracy

Piracy of copyright material on the Internet is an ongoing problem across all media. At Packt, we take the protection of our copyright and licenses very seriously. If you come across any illegal copies of our works, in any form, on the Internet, please provide us with the location address or website name immediately so that we can pursue a remedy.

Please contact us at copyright@impacktpub.com with a link to the suspected pirated material.

We appreciate your help in protecting our authors, and our ability to bring you valuable content.

>1

What is Lean Six Sigma?

This chapter provides an overview of Lean Six Sigma methodology. It should give you a conceptual understanding of the philosophies and the rationale behind two of the most powerful process improvement methodologies in modern management—Lean and Six Sigma. It also puts forward the case for the high impact benefits that a combination of the two approaches can bring, which is far greater than using each of the methodologies alone. This chapter should serve as a brief but useful introduction to Lean Six Sigma for any stakeholder in an organization. It is essential to understand the basic concepts of the Lean Six Sigma methodology before we start the actual implementation. This chapter introduces these concepts, and the subsequent chapters of the book will deal with the actual implementation of Lean Six Sigma.

Six Sigma

Normally denoted as **6 σ**, the term consists of two parts—6 as a number and σ, a Greek letter used as a measure of variation within a specific set of measured data. For a robust process, variation with respect to customer requirements should be as low as possible. A stated Sigma level, in this case 6 Sigma, indicates how much the process varies in meeting customer requirements. The greater the Sigma level, the more the performance of the process coincides with the requirements of the customer. With a greater Sigma level, there are fewer chances of defects within a process, which will ultimately lead to improvements in an organization's bottom line and profitability. As Six Sigma has evolved, the term has acquired various other meanings as well, and refers to a range of issues that can bring benefits to a business. For example, Six Sigma:

> ➤ Is a problem-solving methodology.

> ➤ Is a statistical term to denote a process that generates less than 3.4 defects per million opportunities. This corresponds to a process performing at a quality level of 99.99967 percent.

> ➤ Indicates dramatic improvement levels, typically of more than 50 percent.

> ➤ Involves a distinct organizational infrastructure with a defined skill set, roles, and procedures.

> ➤ Is strongly linked to the bottom-line and the profitability of an organization.

Make a note

The history of Six Sigma

The Six Sigma methodology originated at Motorola in mid 1980s. The story goes that during one of the reviews Bob Galvin, the then CEO, remarked "Our quality stinks." This led Motorola to embark on the quality path known as Six Sigma. The existing basic principles and statistical methods employed in TQM and various quality engineering circles were combined with business and leadership principles to create a holistic management system. This resulted in staggering improvements in the quality level within a few years. Motorola won the inaugural Malcolm Baldridge National Quality Award in 1988. It was then that the world came to know about the secret of their success and thus was born the Six Sigma revolution. By the 1990s, leading corporations such as Texas instruments, Asea Brown Boveri, Allied Signal, Sony Corporation, and General Electric also embraced the methodology and reaped astonishing results. Since then, the legion of the Six Sigma embracing organizations has only grown and includes almost every corporation that one can put a finger on. By 2012, Google returned more than 31,000,000 results related to Six Sigma.

The key concepts of Six Sigma

There are certain key concepts that you need to understand in order to have a good grasp of Six Sigma. This section covers these key concepts.

Accuracy and precision

Accuracy refers to performance with respect to a defined value or target. The closer a value is to its target, the greater its accuracy will be.

Precision refers to the closeness or proximity between various data-points and their relationship to each other. In other words, precision is a measure of variation in measured data. The closer the data points are to each other, the greater the precision and the less the variation.

The following figure elucidates the difference further:

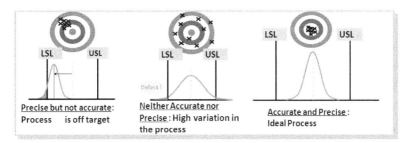

The accuracy of a measured set of data is indicated by measuring central tendency metrics such as the mean, mode, or the median. Variation is the *voice of the process* and is indicated by measures of dispersion such as Standard Deviation.

Y=f(x)

This equation is at the heart of Six Sigma. This simply indicates that *Y* or the outcome or effect of a process is a function of or dependent on various factors or causes, referred to as *Xs*. In other words, certain sets of inputs called *X* are transformed by a function, *f*, into an output called *Y*. The following table explains the relationship between *Y* and *X*.

Y	X
Dependent variable	Independent variable
Output/result	Input/process
Effect	Cause
Symptom	Problem
Monitor	Control

Instead of focusing on effects that would be akin to tackling symptoms rather than the root cause, the methodology stresses the identification and manipulation of underlying causes or *Xs* for these effects, *Ys*. The *Y* still needs to be monitored but *Xs* need to be controlled. This focus results in a sustained improvement with long terms benefits instead of superficial, flash-in-the-pan improvement with a risk of recurrence of the problem.

Focus on defects and variation

As mentioned earlier, Six Sigma is customer-centric. The term **defect** is used to denote instances or events that fail to deliver as per the requirements that are most critical to the customer, called **critical to quality (CTQ)**. Every defect in the process has an adverse impact not only on the quality but also on the time the process takes to be both carried out and reworked. This results in an additional cost, which often goes unnoticed but impacts overall profitability. Any measurable event that may result in a defect is called an **opportunity**. A Six Sigma process technically implies 3.4 **defects per million opportunities (DPMO)** in that process.

The Six Sigma methodology also focuses on reducing variation in a given process. As seen in the following figure, the variation in the process reduces dramatically with the increase in Sigma level. A particular Sigma level indicates the distance between the target and the customer specification for the process, so the higher the Sigma level, the closer this will be. The target of a process is the value on which it is supposed to be centered.

A Six Sigma process implies that the process has been designed to be twice as good as the customer specification. Technically, it implies that the customer specifications are six standard deviations away from the process target. In other words, the variation is so low that six such processes can be accommodated within this gap between the process target and the specification limits. If we define defects as the outputs that fall out of the specification limits, we can see that as the sigma levels go up, there would be fewer chances of such defects being generated.

Make a note

Variation is inherent in all processes. It cannot be eliminated. We can only ensure that these variations are within our control. Six Sigma focuses on reducing variation to be within acceptable limits.

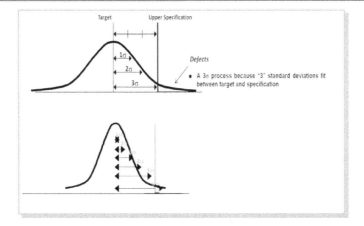

Here we can see the way the Sigma level and variation in a process relate to one another—as the Sigma level increases, the degree of variation decreases.

Exponential improvement

Six Sigma as a methodology can lead to exponential improvement (as we see in the previous image). As the Sigma level goes up, the scale of improvement goes up dramatically. The following two graphics also demonstrate how improvement dramatically increases along with the Sigma level:

σ	DPMO	% Yield
6	3.4	99.99967
5	233	99.9767
4	6,210	99.379
3	66,807	93.3193
2	308,537	69.1463
Process Capability	Defects Per Million Opportunities	% Yield

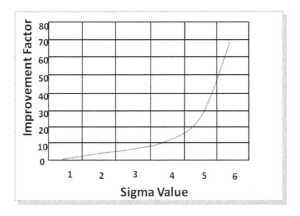

Three Dimensions

Six Sigma has three dimensions to address all the requirements of a specific process—**design**, **improvement**, and **management**. It addresses all these dimensions with specific methodologies such as Design for Six Sigma (DFSS), DMAIC, and Process Management.

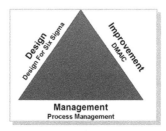

The DFSS approach is used when a defined process is not in place or no further significant improvement is possible in the process. In this case, we need to design a robust process afresh. The DMAIC approach is used to help an existing and defined process to perform at its optimal level and to meet customer requirements. Process management refers to the routine approach to ensure that the existing process operates at the current and sustainable levels. This book deals with the more popular DMAIC approach.

Advantages of Six Sigma

Six Sigma brings certain unique advantages such as:

➤ An emphasis on the identification of opportunities and elimination of defects according to the customer's requirements

➤ A focus on reducing process variation

➤ Addressing accuracy and consistency in a process

➤ Employing data and statistics to drive decisions

➤ Incorporating a comprehensive set of quality tools under a powerful framework

➤ Prescribing a company-wide cultural transformation to achieve sustained improvements

Lean

Lean, as the name suggests, is about identifying and eliminating the "flab" or waste in a process thereby improving the speed of it. Lean considers spending any kind of resource that does not add any value to the end customer, to achieve an outcome as waste. This waste needs to be eliminated to speed up the process and improve overall efficiency. Unlike Six Sigma, which addresses accuracy and consistency through its focus on reducing defects and variation in the process, Lean addresses the speed, time, and efficiency of a process through the elimination of waste.

Make a note

The history of Lean

Post World War II, the Japanese industry in general was grappling with a plethora of problems. There was no market. They had to compete against western companies that enjoyed economy of scale. There were severe credit restrictions imposed by occupying forces leading to non-availability of capital to invest in new plants. Organizations like Toyota were struggling to stay afloat. It was this gloomy backdrop that prompted Taichi Ohno, an executive at Toyota to redesign the production system. His vision was focussed on how to maximize the returns on limited investment. It zeroed down to three fundamental principles – i) Build only what is required, ii) Eliminate anything that does not add value, and iii) Stop if something goes wrong. These ideas along with total employee involvement formed the core of the famous Toyota Production system that catapulted Toyota from the brink of bankruptcy to the pedestal of industry leader. As Toyota and other large Japanese companies expanded worldwide, the world gradually came to know of the Toyota Production system that gradually evolved into Lean manufacturing. Now, the Lean principles have grown beyond traditional manufacturing and have been employed in diverse industries such as service and software.

Key concepts of Lean

You now have an understanding of the core concepts behind Six Sigma; you now need to do the same thing with Lean before you can try to bring them together.

Waste

As mentioned earlier, **waste** is anything that is part of a process, by design or by accident, that does not add any value in the eyes of the customer. Lean aims at identifying and eliminating waste from a specific process.

A quick mnemonic to remember waste in a process would be **TIMWOODS**: Transportation, Inventory, Motion, Waiting, Over-production, Over-processing, Defects, and (underutilized) Skills. We will go into more detail on these later in the book.

Value and non-value adding activities

A **value-added activity** in a process is something that a customer would agree is essential for the end product or service. The activities that do not fulfill this criterion are called **non-value adding activities**. The proportion of value-added activities in any given process is an indicator of the efficiency of the process. Our aim, with Lean, is to eliminate non-value adding activities from a process and hence improve its speed and efficiency.

Process cycle efficiency

Process cycle efficiency is a metric that can be used to identify an area in which the efficiency of a process could be improved. It is defined by the ratio of the time taken by value-adding tasks to the total time it takes to carry out the process.

Process velocity

Process velocity is an indicator of the flexibility of a process. Flexibility refers to the ability of a process to respond to potential changes in a cost-effective manner. It is calculated as the number of activities in the process divided by the total time taken to complete the process, known as **process lead time**. Process lead time is directly proportional to the number of activities within a process. Hence if we eliminate non-value adding activities, the process velocity goes up automatically, thereby improving flexibility.

Advantages of Lean

Lean brings certain unique advantages such as:

➤ A focus on process velocity

➤ Identifying value-adding and non-value adding activities from the customer's point of view

➤ Helping to identify delays in a process

➤ Helping to simplify the process

The concept of Lean Six Sigma

As you will have probably already noticed, the effectiveness of a combined approach takes improvements to dramatically different levels. Lean and Six Sigma complement each other perfectly. Six Sigma not only scores in areas that require reduction in variation and the removal of defects but also cultivates a robust culture to drive sustained organizational improvements. Lean, on the other hand, is very effective at increasing the efficiency and speed of a process. Combined, the Lean Six Sigma approach enjoys the strengths of both methodologies, while overcoming their respective disadvantages. Lean Six Sigma is undoubtedly the most effective and proven improvement methodology in recent times.

Methodology / Parameter	Accuracy	Consistency	Speed	Time	Efficiency
Six Sigma	Y	Y	N	N	N
Lean	N	N	Y	Y	Y
Lean Six Sigma	Y	Y	Y	Y	Y

Case study

The following is an example case study that will be used throughout the book to demonstrate the effectiveness of Lean Six Sigma for an organization when applied successfully. This scenario should help to elucidate the tools, techniques, and key concepts of Lean Six Sigma, which should help you implement it successfully in your organization.

ABC Inc., an IT services company, has lately realized that it is losing its ground to the competition. Based on industry data and other studies, it found that the customer satisfaction with the support services has been just or below average. The customer satisfaction rating was found to be 70% while the ratings for "average" and "best-in-class" companies were 75% and 83% respectively. They also observed that there is a strong positive correlation between the customer satisfaction rating and new account growth. The average cost per support call of ABC Inc. was also found to be significantly higher at $25 compared to $22 and $18 for average and best-in-class companies. The management team then concluded that a Lean Six Sigma improvement project should be launched to improve the customer satisfaction rating and to reduce the cost per support call. The management strongly feels that this will help them control operational costs as well as achieve higher account growth. A Lean Six Sigma team was constituted to drive this.

Summary

Six Sigma has been successfully deployed across organizations all around the world. It is a data-driven methodology built around a framework to identify and reduce defects and variation in critical organization processes. It addresses the accuracy and consistency of these processes. Six Sigma also helps to build a culture of continuous improvement through its prescriptive framework.

Lean originated in a manufacturing setup but its concepts have found application across a range of industries. Unlike Six Sigma, it addresses the speed and efficiency of a process by identifying waste and eliminating non-value adding activities from it. This also helps simplify it. Studies have shown that the **cost of poor quality,** the cost associated with defective products or services, increases as the number of steps or the complexity of a process increases. Probability of defects being generated goes up as the number of steps increase. This results in greater reworking, and this of course costs money.

Lean Six Sigma is a combined approach that utilizes the strengths of the two methodologies. The two approaches complement each other well. By combining the two approaches, organizations and businesses will find dramatic improvements.

The next chapter describes the life cycle and process of implementing Lean Six Sigma in an organization.

Quiz

1. Which of the following statements is true about Six Sigma quality?

    a.   Motorola invented Six Sigma methodology

    b.   Six Sigma implies 3.4 defects per million opportunities

    c.   Six Sigma is a statistics and data-driven methodology

    d.   All of the above

2. Which of the following statements is not correct?

    a.   Accuracy is indicated by measures of central tendency

    b.   Precision implies the gap between actual and target performances

    c.   Precision is measured by standard deviation

    d.   Precision is an indication of variation within the process

3. The equation Y=f(X) is at the core of Six Sigma methodology. Which of these statements is not correct?

    a.   Y is a dependent variable and X is an independent variable

    b.   Y is an independent variable and X is a dependent variable

    c.   Y should be controlled and X should be monitored

    d.   Both B and C

4. Which of these statements is correct in view of Lean principles?

    a.   Waste is any non-value added activity in a process that should be eliminated

    b.   Process cycle efficiency is an indicator of the time taken by value added activities as the percentage of the total process time

    c.   The lower the number of steps in a process, the higher the velocity of the process

    d.   All of the above

5. Six Sigma does not focus on:

    a.   Reduction of defects

    b.   Improving the cost of poor quality

    c.   Reduction of variation

    d.   Eliminate NVA

6. Lean does not focus on:

    a.   Reduction of variation

    b.   Eliminating waste

    c.   Reduction of defects

    d.   Improvement in process velocity

7. Sigma Level indicates:
   a. Closeness of process performance to the customer requirements
   b. Variation in the process
   c. Capability of the process
   d. All of the above

8. Lean Six Sigma methodology:
   a. Is applicable only for manufacturing organizations
   b. Has cost saving as the primary objective
   c. Has not been effective in service organizations
   d. None of the above

Answers: 1 – D; 2 – B; 3 – D; 4 – D; 5 – D; 6 – C; 7 – D; 8 - D

>2

Planning the Implementation

This chapter provides you with a blueprint for the implementation of Lean Six Sigma in your organization. It discusses the roles, skills, training, and governance mechanisms needed for the successful deployment of a Lean Six Sigma initiative. More than that, it will also show you how to sustain the results of the initiative, and how to move it across your organization.

Life cycle of Lean Six Sigma

The Lean Six Sigma implementation lifecycle can be divided into a five step process. These steps are **initiate, enable**, **implement**, **replicate,** and **sustain**. The following diagram gives you a visual demonstration of the step-by-step process and what each stage involves. By breaking it down into these five steps, the process becomes more manageable and implementation is more effective.

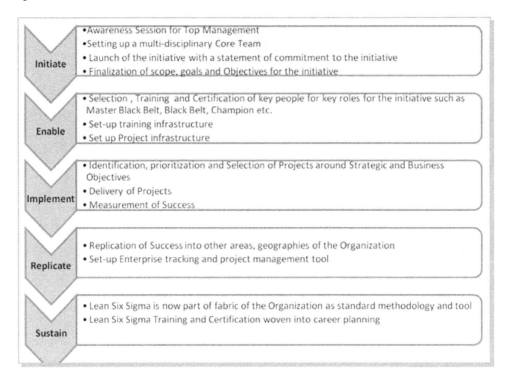

Initiate (days 1-2)

A Lean Six Sigma initiative requires preparation and planning like any other large-scale program. Typically, this will involve setting up a core or "steering" team with a support infrastructure. The top management and senior leaders in an organization will undergo comprehensive awareness training, providing them with an overview of the Lean Six Sigma deployment process and explaining the challenges and expectations such a project will entail. Certain macro issues such as scope, timeframe, goals, and objectives are also dealt with at this stage. The executive team also issues a statement of commitment to the initiative. This step can be completed in about 2-3 days.

Enable (days 3-8)

Once there is clarity and commitment from the top management and goals and objectives are put in place, the second step, **Enable**, involves the selection and training of key people who will actually drive the initiative. Some organizations may seek the help of an external consultant who works closely with these key people to deploy the initiative, especially during the initial days. The key roles in Lean Six Sigma are:

➤ **Deployment leader**: They own the vision, direction, integration, and results and lead the cultural change associated with the initiative. As stated earlier, they define the scope, goals, and objectives for the initiative.

➤ **Core team**: This is generally a multi-disciplinary team comprising business leaders from functions such as Human Resources, Finance, Information Technology, and Training. The responsibility of the core team is to provide the necessary support infrastructure for the success of the initiative.

➤ **Financial representative**: This person is responsible for setting up standard guidelines for monetary valuation of project improvements. They also check the Lean Six Sigma results.

➤ **Champion**: This is typically a business leader of a unit, division, or region, who owns the success or failure of the project. They maintain the link between business strategy and projects, and identify and assign Black Belts (see later in this list) to projects. They are responsible for removing roadblocks to the project's success.

➤ **Sponsor or process owner:** Responsible for the solutions of the project delivered by the Lean Six Sigma team. They work closely with the Champion and the Lean Six Sigma team to identify and drive the improvement project. They are also responsible for providing resource support in the form of team members for the project.

➤ **Master Black Belt (MBB)**: They have the highest level of knowledge on Lean Six Sigma and act as a guide for the Black Belts who drive the project. They work closely with the Champion to ensure the smooth deployment of methodology. They also develop the training curriculum on Lean Six Sigma, and play a key role in the project closure process.

➤ **Black Belt (BB)**: This is a full-time practitioner of Lean Six Sigma methodology and a facilitator or leader of the Lean Six Sigma project team. With a high level of skill in methodology, they play a major role in ensuring that the project meets its goal. They are also well rounded in communication, change management, and problem-solving skills.

➤ **Green Belt (GB)**: These are local advocates of the initiative and are generally part-time practitioners of smaller-scope projects associated with their regular work. They also assist Black Belts in driving Lean Six Sigma projects locally.

➤ **Yellow / White Belts (YB / WB)**: Like Green Belts, they focus on smaller-scope projects limited to a specific area. However, they are a lower skill level than Green Belts.

The following diagram provides you with a visual representation of the hierarchy of roles involved in Lean Six Sigma initiatives:

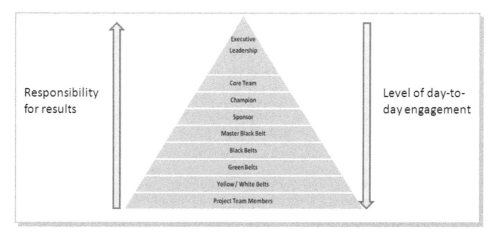

Before we go on to the next step, it is worth clarifying certain possible misconceptions about Lean Six Sigma roles.

Roles are not mutually exclusive. An individual can perform different roles at the same time. For example, a senior executive or a champion can also serve as the Green Belt depending on the need. In many organizations, training and certifications around various Lean Six Sigma levels is seen as a good way to enhance leadership skills and to develop future leaders.

Roles have no necessary relationship with the hierarchy of the organization. Positions within the organizational hierarchy do not necessarily correlate with the Lean Six Sigma roles. Master Black Belts and Black Belts may report to a senior executive who may be a Green Belt. These roles are indicators of the level of training and expertise on Lean Six Sigma methodology rather than an individual's position within the organization.

Typical distribution of various belts

A question that typically comes up during implementation is with respect to the number of Master Black Belts, Black Belts, Green Belts, and Yellow Belts in the organization. These roles require intensive and specialized training and some of these roles are full-time roles. An organization would need to understand the effort and costs associated with this. In a Lean Six Sigma organization, the typical strength of various belts in relation to the rest of the organization and other belts are listed in the following table. This information should provide you with a guideline to decide the allocation of resources in the Lean Six Sigma initiative.

Certification level	% of organization strength	Typical supervision ratio
Master Black Belt (MBB)	1%	MBB:BB = 1:5
Black Belt (BB)	3-5%	BB:GB = 1:3-5
Green Belt (GB)	10-20%	
Yellow / White Belt (YB/WB)	50-75%	--

Implementing your projects (day 9 onwards)

Projects are at the heart of a Lean Six Sigma initiative. Projects are identified, prioritized, and implemented to improve a company's performance; ultimately it should yield financial benefits. The projects must be clearly defined for improvements to be realized. For maximum impact, projects should be linked to the strategic business objectives of the organization. A crucial distinction between any project and a Lean Six Sigma project is that the latter generally addresses problems whose solutions are not known. A simple and effective index, as suggested by Thomas Pyzdek, in the *Six Sigma Handbook* (McGraw-Hill, 2003), is the **Pareto Priority Index (PPI)**.

Make a note

PPI = (Savings * Probability of Success) / (Cost*Time to Complete the Project)

The values of various terms in the formula would only be indicative and need not be very accurate. All the projects are selected based on PPI. The higher the PPI, the higher is the priority of the project.

The following table provides an example of how to use PPI. Here, three hypothetical projects have been prioritized using PPI.

Project	Saving ($'000)	Probability	Cost ($'000)	Time (days)	PPI
Accounts receivable	300	0.9	10	120	0.225
Customer satisfaction	450	0.75	15	180	0.125
Accuracy	360	0.8	5	140	0.411

In this case, the project on accuracy with a PPI of 0.411 gets the topmost priority, followed by accounts receivable and customer satisfaction.

The savings from a Lean Six Sigma Project can be broadly classified as: a) hard savings b) soft savings and c) cost avoidance. These different categories work in different ways and also impact on different aspects of the company's success.

This table provides you with an easy guide to the three different savings categories of Lean Six Sigma and where their results have an impact:

Saving category	Definition	Example	Impact
Hard saving	Direct cost, tangible recurring expenses	Fewer people to perform same activity; less money spent to carry out a task	Bottom-line
Soft saving	Enhanced process capacity to do more with less or with same	Reduced turn-around time, improved efficiency	Efficiency, capacity enhancement in
Cost avoidance	Avoiding any anticipated cost or investment	Avoiding purchase of additional equipment, avoiding investment in infrastructure	Future

After the selection of a project, a team is identified to run the project and to use the Lean Six Sigma methodology to provide a solution to the targeted problem and to ultimately improve an organization's performance.

Green Belt and Black Belt projects

Lean Six Sigma projects are typically classified as Green Belt and Black Belt projects. There are several criteria to distinguish between the two:

> **Use of resources**: Green Belt projects tend to have less reach and do not require extensive organizational resources or capital investment to drive gains. On the other hand, a Black Belt project deals with much more complex issues at an organizational level that may involve the participation of cross-functional teams and may require substantial capital investment for benefits to be realized.

> **Use of statistical tools**: Green Belt projects generally employ basic statistical tools. Black Belt projects, on the other hand, utilize much more advanced statistical tools.

> **CTQ**: Green Belt projects typically will have one CTQ with few factors. Black Belt projects will have more than one CTQ with a large number of factors.

Before the implementation of projects it helps to understand what kind of project is being carried out. This is crucial with respect to what kind of resources and efforts would be needed to carry out the project. This will also help in defining the scope and spread of the project.

Replicate (ongoing)

As the organization experiences success with the implementation of a project in one area, it will want to replicate the experience in other areas. However, introducing the initiative into each new area is akin to launching an initiative afresh and involves the five steps of implementation that we have been discussing. However, knowledge from previous experience will be useful even when you are customizing the initiative in different areas. Also, as more and more projects are implemented, the organization will have to set up a system enabling it to track and manage the development of the various projects that are being run. As the initiative matures, and as more and more projects are successfully implemented, the next step, sustain, sets in.

Sustain (ongoing)

As the Lean Six Sigma practice grows, it becomes increasingly woven into the fabric of the organization. It is no longer an initiative but is now part of the organization's process. A regular review of the projects and the overall program helps to keep the practice relevant to the strategic and business objectives of the organization. Lean Six Sigma is now used as a high impact and fast-result tool to address issues that crop up in the organization. Training and refresher training sessions are conducted for new employees and existing staff to enable them to address problems in their respective areas. Lean Six Sigma related skills and certifications become part of the job and role description repository of the organization and may be used as tools to identify and develop future leadership skills within the organization.

Project and program review

The projects that have been identified and are being implemented need to be reviewed regularly to ensure that they are on track and to remove roadblocks if there are any. Reviews are an essential part of sustaining the Lean Six Sigma initiative.

There are two key types of review: **project review** and **program review**. The project review is usually conducted at monthly intervals; the program review, involving the meanwhile, is conducted less regularly at quarterly intervals. Project review entails the review of milestones of different stages of a project—*define, measure, analyze, improve, and control*—and roadblocks faced during various stages. Program review is used to review if the overall initiative is progressing in the right direction. The various parameters that can be an indicator of the effectiveness of the program are the number of projects registered, the number of projects closed, employee participation, training effectiveness, return on investment, and savings realized.

The table below shows you the key distinctions between a project and a program review and the suggested parameters that may be considered in the respective reviews:

Review	Suggested parameters for review
Project	■ Stage ■ Deliverables ■ Roadblocks, if any
Program	■ Number of projects registered ■ Number of projects closed ■ Number of projects abandoned ■ Employee participation ■ Training feedback ■ Gross and net savings realized ■ Return on investment

Communication

It is very important to communicate the success stories and results with the organization as a whole to sustain energy and enthusiasm for the initiative. This can be done at all levels within an organization through e-mails, newsletters, or notice boards. Celebrations around key milestones also send positive messages around the initiative. Another useful idea is to set up idea factories or idea banks to attract ideas and contributions from employees across the organization. Many organizations run various idea generating campaigns around certain themes in which employees participate and contribute ideas and suggestions. This results in not only a collection of bright and novel ideas but also improves employee engagement.

As highlighted earlier, the implementation stage onwards are ongoing processes and would go beyond 30 days. The DMAIC methodology, tools, and techniques involved in a Lean Six Sigma project are discussed in the subsequent chapters.

Summary

As we have seen so far, the Lean Six Sigma implementation lifecycle is typically a five step process: *initiate, enable, implement, replicate, and sustain*. For the initiative to be successful, it is essential to have complete commitment from the senior management in the organization.

The various roles in a Lean Six Sigma implementation ensure that the delineation of responsibilities and tasks within a given project is clear. In turn, this should ensure that the implementation of the project is frictionless, as everyone knows what they are doing and should thus work together efficiently and effectively.

It is absolutely essential that the projects that comprise your Lean Six Sigma initiative are linked to the strategic and business objectives of your organization – after all, your organization is the reason that you're implementing the initiative in the first place! By using criteria such as the Pareto Priority Index, you can ensure that the initiative is not only working in line with the objectives of your organization, but also driving improvement, going beyond those objectives.

Even if you have successfully aligned your Lean Six Sigma projects with your business objectives, you need to ensure that the initiative and the improvements that it should be driving are sustained and replicated throughout different areas of your organization. This is why the review is an integral part of the process; indeed, it is something that you should bear in mind throughout the entire process, as it is only by reviewing the success of the projects in place that you can refine, adapt, and improve even more.

The chapters that follow will describe the DMAIC methodology and tools and techniques associated with Lean Six Sigma in greater detail. The next chapter will specifically deal with the first phase of DMAIC: *define*. The define stage should further guarantee the clarity of your projects and will thus also ensure that the alignment between business objectives and your Lean Six Sigma project is perfect. Your are now well on your way to fully implementing Lean Six Sigma—so keep going, there's no time like the present!

Quiz

Test yourself on what you have read in the chapter with this quick quiz.

1. Which of the following statements about Pareto Priority Index (PPI) is true?
    a. The values in the PPI formula are only indicative and need not be very accurate
    b. It is used to prioritize improvement projects
    c. The higher the PPI, the higher the priority for the project
    d. All of the above

2. In a mature Lean Six Sigma program:
    a. The Quality department is the sole custodian of the program
    b. Nearly everyone in the organization is involved in some way at some time
    c. Only a small number of employees are involved and that too only for limited period of time
    d. Projects do not add any further value

3. Black Belts are:
    a. Well rounded in communication, change management, and problem-solving skills
    b. Primarily technical experts in the methodology
    c. Full time personnel
    d. All the above

4. The management team wants to prioritize and evaluate one project out of the following projects. Which project should they go with?

Project	Saving ($'000)	Probability	Cost ($'000)	Time (days)
A	500	0.8	75	120
B	1200	0.6	215	150
C	900	0.5	175	150
D	1000	0.7	180	180

    a. A
    b. B
    c. C
    a. D

5. Which of the following is a saving category for a Lean Six Sigma project?
    a. Cost avoidance
    b. Hard saving
    c. Soft saving
    d. All the above

6. A project to reduce the process cycle time has been initiated with an objective of reducing personnel cost per unit. Which of these can constitute a valid saving?
    a. An increase in revenue without any reduction of number of personnel
    b. Excess personnel removed from the process
    c. Excess personnel is reassigned somewhere else
    d. Any of the above

7. Which of these statements is not correct with respect to roles in a Lean Six Sigma program?
    a. Roles are mutually exclusive
    b. Roles are strictly in line with the organization hierarchy
    c. Both A and B
    d. Only A

8. For a Lean Six Sigma deployment the preferred plan for training employees is to:
    a. Train everyone in the organization at the same time
    b. Train the supervisors and team leaders who manage the large proportion of personnel
    c. Start with the top management
    d. Create awareness with the customer

Answers: 1 – D; 2 – B; 3 – D; 4 - A; 5 – D; 6 – D; 7 – C; 8 - C

> 3

Define (Days 9-11)

This chapter describes the first stage, Define, of the DMAIC methodology. Defining is one of the most crucial stages as it decides the direction of the project. The Define stage establishes a foundation that helps the subsequent stages to follow the structure of the methodology and to yield the desired results. This chapter will describe what the Define stage should deliver, along with the tools and techniques needed to do so. We will also return to the case study introduced in *Chapter 1*, *What is Lean Six Sigma?*, to illustrate how the Define stage should work.

Define: key deliverables. Define is the cornerstone of the DMAIC journey and plays a crucial role in the project lifecycle. The value of the Define stage can be summed up by a much repeated adage: *A problem well stated is a problem half-solved*. The Define stage creates the foundation over which a project can be built; it enables the subsequent phases to be executed effectively. The key deliverables of Define are:

- ➤ Project charter
- ➤ Voice of customer
- ➤ Preliminary high level process map
- ➤ Team formation

Let's explore these deliverables in detail.

Project charter (day 9)

The project charter is a document created by and shared within the project team, and it documents the Lean Six Sigma Project objectives, goals, financial benefits, scope, and tentative timeline. It also identifies the team working on the project. The key elements of a project charter are as follows:

> **Business case**: The business case is the reason and rationale behind doing the project. It is a sort of executive summary or elevator speech about why the project is important and how it is linked to the overall strategy and objectives of the organization. Alignment of the strategic goals of the organization and the project is critical to the success of the program and the business. Generally, the champion or sponsor defines the business case. A few guiding questions to help create a good business case are:

> > Why should the project be done?

> > Why now and not later?

> > What are the potential risks if the project is not done now?

> > What is the potential impact on the business objectives?

> > What is the financial impact?

> **Problem statement**: The problem statement basically answers the question, "What is the pain point that this project is going to address?". A well written problem statement needs to be:

> > **Clear and concise**: It should not be more than two sentences long. It should use simple language that is understood by all the team members.

> > **Specific**: It should be very specific with respect to what the pain point is exactly: where does it occur? When does it occur? What is the negative impact of the pain and what is the opportunity once the pain is addressed? A project should ideally tackle only one pain point at a time.

> > **Independent of causes or blames**: It should avoid jumping to conclusions about causes and assigning blame.

Make a note

A poor problem statement would be: Employees report late to work, which results in poor productivity.

A good problem statement would instead be: At the XYZ unit, about 48% of employees report to work 20-25 minutes late in each of the three shifts, leading to about a 15% drop in productivity.

- ➤ **Goal statement**: A goal statement describes the expected outcome of the project. A good goal statement follows the SMART guidelines:

    - ➢ **Specific**: It should be very specific with respect to what you want to achieve. Ideally, a goal statement should not involve more than one expected outcome.

    - ➢ **Measurable**: The expected outcome should be quantifiable and measurable. An outcome that cannot be quantified or measured is vague and lacks focus.

    - ➢ **Attainable**: The outcome should strike a balance between a "stretch" target and an "easily achieved" target.

    - ➢ **Relevant**: It should be relevant to the pain described in the problem statement. It should "speak" to the problem statement.

    - ➢ **Time-bound**: It should provide the time by which the outcome is expected. The time should be set reasonably.

    A good goal statement starts with an action, for example, *to reduce, to increase, to enhance, to improve*, and so on (see the following box). At times, the goal statement may be revised if the analysis of the Voice of Customer suggests that there are new requirements.

Make a note

A poor example of a goal statement would be something like: we will reduce the number of latecomers to achieve target productivity.

A much better way to write that would be: To bring down the percentage of employees who report to work 20-25 minutes late from 48% to 10% within 3 months.

- ➤ **Project scope**: The project scope decides the boundaries of the project. It describes what is included and what is not included in the project. The project scope needs to strike a balance between being too broad and being too narrow. If the scope of the project is too broad, its success will be diluted, whereas if it is too narrow, you may get sub-optimized improvement results. The project scope may also be seen as a mutually agreed upon contract between the project team and business area or unit for which the project is being driven so that the team can keep itself focused.

- ➤ **Financial benefits**: The project charter also outlines the financial impact that the project should bring when it has been carried out successfully. At the start of the project, this is a tentative ball-park figure that may undergo revision as the team progresses through the different stages.

- ➤ **Timeline**: The project charter provides a roadmap of the DMAIC stages with a schedule or timeline for the completion of each of these stages.

- ➤ **Team**: The last part of the project charter is the section that provides information on the team members working on the project along with their specified roles.

The information in a project charter is preliminary and may undergo revision as greater clarity on the goals, the timescale, and the financial impact emerge with the progress of the project. In other words, a project charter is a live document that requires numerous revisits.

A typical project charter may look something like this:

Project code					
Project title					
Project start date			Project completion date		
Project team	Name			Role	
Sponsor				CTQ	
Business case					
Problem statement					
Goal statement					
Project scope	Within			Outside	
Timeline	Define	Measure	Analyze	Improve	Control
	Start	Start	Start	Start	Start
	End	End	End	End	End
Financial benefit ($) and justification					

Voice of customer (day 10)

Lean Six Sigma as a methodology starts with an effort to understand customer requirements and finishes with the fulfillment of these requirements. It sounds simple but it can be easy to lose sight of this when talking about the details of methodologies such as Lean and Six Sigma. First, we need to understand who the customer at the end of the process is: *A customer is a recipient of the output of a process.* A customer may be an external agency outside the organization or an internal agency within the organization.

It is crucial to gather information about customer requirements through various mechanisms such as feedback surveys, complaint data, directly speaking to the customer, and market research data. Often, these requirements are vague and non-specific, but it is nevertheless important to engage with these requirements. However, to ensure that you act effectively on the feedback, it is also important to translate these requirements into something measurable. These are known as **Critical-to-Quality (CTQ)** requirements, and they need to be acknowledged before any improvement can be initiated. For example, a customer of a pizza company may complain that it takes too long for their pizza to be delivered. This could be translated into a CTQ by rephrasing it like this: "The order needs to be delivered within 30 minutes of being placed."

A logical sequence of analyzing the voice of customer and creating CTQ would be:

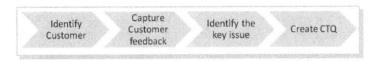

Here are a few examples of this process:

Customer	Type of customer	Voice of customer	Key issue	CTQ
XYZ	External	It always take ages to connect to the right person	Time taken to reach the right connect is long	Time taken to connect to right person to be less than or equal to 30 seconds
ABC	External	It takes very long to get my pizza	Time elapsed between order placed and delivered is long	Time from order placed to delivery should be less than or equal to 15 minutes

Voice of customer should be central to your projects—listen carefully to what the customer is saying, but remember to translate what is being said into something measurable and actionable.

High-level process map (day 11)

A high level process map is drawn to bring clarity to the project definition so the team members of the project understand what they are working towards. A common and useful tool to develop a process map is called a **SIPOC diagram**. The purpose of a SIPOC diagram is to create a high-level representation of the process under study without getting into the details of it. Detailed process maps will be created in the later stages of DMAIC. SIPOC stands for Supplier, Inputs, Process, Output, and Customer, and provides the details of how each of these aspects interacts in the project in one diagram. The steps to create a SIPOC are as follows:

1. Outline the major steps of the process as block diagrams. A good rule of thumb is to have no more than four to six steps. Action words should be used to describe the process steps. Decide the start and the stop points of the process. A process is nothing but a series of activities that transforms inputs into outputs.

2. Identify the outputs of the process. There may be one or multiple outputs of a process and they may include both tangible as well as intangible outputs. Tangible outputs have a physical existence, usually taking the form of physical products, documents, and reports. Intangible outputs, meanwhile, do not have a physical existence; they are not discernible through one or more senses, for example, customer satisfaction, knowledge, technical know-how, strategic information, goodwill, and so on.

3. Identify the customers. A customer is the recipient of the outputs of the process.

4. Identify the inputs of the process. There may be one or multiple inputs that go into the process.

5. Identify the agencies that supply these inputs. These agencies may be internal or external. It may also happen that suppliers are the recipients (or customers) of outputs of the process.

A visual representation of SIPOC looks like this:

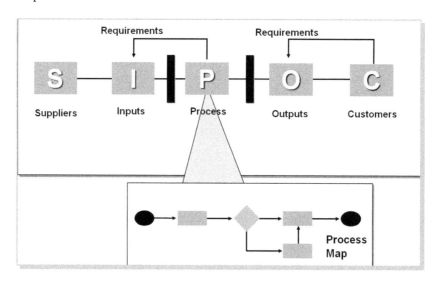

SIPOC is a good place to begin a project as it helps the team create a visual representation of the process and the related stakeholders, inputs, and outputs of the process.

Form team (day 11)

First of all, we need to identify the key stakeholders of the process that needs to be improved. The key stakeholders are those who are necessary for the success of the project. The team is formed with members representing these key stakeholders. These representatives should be held in high esteem by their group as well as the other stakeholders. Ideally, for effective team management, a typical Lean Six Sigma project team should not have more than six to seven full-time members.

Almost all teams go through the following stages of development:

➤ **Forming**: The team sets procedures and protocols. Interaction between members is tentative and polite. The team leader dominates this stage.

➤ **Storming**: This stage witnesses conflicts between team members. Team members question authority with respect to team objectives, structure, process, and protocols. The team members try to define their role in the team.

➤ **Norming**: The team members begin taking responsibility or ownership of the goals, rules, and behavior. The team works together. The norms for the group are defined and enforced.

➤ **Performing**: In this final stage, the team members contribute to the success of the team and take pride in being part of the success of the team.

An awareness of these stages is of great help while managing the dynamics within the team. The different roles within the team may be specified as follows:

➤ **Team leader**: The team leader's job is to keep the focus of the team on the project objective. They are also a facilitator and should work closely with the other team members to ensure that the project is on track. They should have the ability to inspire and influence people. Ideally, the stakeholder with maximum stake in the improvement of the process should serve as the team leader.

➤ **Black Belt**: The Black Belt provides the team with the knowledge of the Lean Six Sigma methodology and helps the team with the proper application of tools and the correct interpretation of results of these tools.

➤ **Team members**: The rest of the team work as team members. They bring together their knowledge, experience, ideas, and viewpoints. Some of the team members may also work as scribe and coordinator to capture the various minutes of meetings and to coordinate the tasks and activities assigned to respective team members.

The details of the team and the roles will be incorporated into the project charter.

Checklist

The following checklist lists the deliverables and documents that need to be in place at the end of the Define stage:

Deliverable	Status	
Project charter	Yes	No
Voice of customer and CTQ	Yes	No
SIPOC	Yes	No
Team formation	Yes	No

Case study – the Define stage

Here is the Define stage for the case study that we first saw in *Chapter 1, What is Lean Six Sigma?* The project charter and the SIPOC are provided in the following table:

Project Charter:

Project code	1234			
Project title	Improving Customer Satisfaction Rating			
Project start date	15th January 2010	Project completion date	15th May 2010	
Project team	Name		Role	
	Christopher Rowe		Team leader	
	Amanda Kerr		Team member	
	Jonathan Kerry		Team member	
	Robert Spencer		Team member	
	Keith Antony		Black Belt	
Sponsor	Andrew Broad		CTQ	Customer satisfaction
Business case	The customer satisfaction rating has been below average and there is a strong correlation between the customer satisfaction rating and the new account growth. We need to improve our customer satisfaction ratings to remain competitive. An increase in our new business growth from 1 percent to 4 percent (or better) would increase our gross revenues by about $4 million. Our cost per support call is also significantly higher at $25 compared to those of average and best-in-class companies at $22 and $18 respectively. Maintaining the support cost per call at the current levels, this can help us realize a net gain of at least $3 million.			
Problem statement	The customer satisfaction rating of 70% is lower than the competition. The ratings for "average" and "best-in-class" companies are 75% and 83% respectively.			

Goal statement	To improve customer satisfaction rating from its current level, that is 70% to 83% by 30th April 2010				
Project scope	Within: IT support calls			Outside: Calls excluding IT support calls	
Timeline	Define	Measure	Analyze	Improve	Control
	Start	Start	Start	Start	Start
	01-15-10	01-18-10	01-22-10	03-20-10	04-15-10
	End	End	End	End	End
	01-17-10	02-04-10	03-19-10	04-14-10	05-15-10
Financial benefit ($) and justification	3 million USD. This is a tentative saving assuming that the cost per support call is maintained at the current levels. This can even increase if we are able to reduce this cost.				

SIPOC:

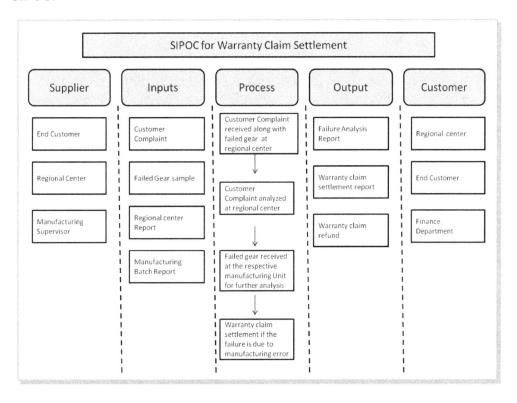

Summary

The Define stage is the most crucial part of the improvement project lifecycle as it provides the foundation over which the subsequent stages of DMAIC will be built. *A problem well stated is a problem half-solved.*

The Define stage involves the creation of a project charter. The project charter will be essential throughout the process as it is the document that will provide information about the improvement project. It will include information such as the business case, the problem statement, the goal statement, the scope, the financial impact of the project as well as the team working on it. It provides clarity and uniform understanding about the project to the team, which will be integral to the project's success. The map helps to sharpen this clarity further.

Possibly the most important thing to do at this early stage is to capture the voice of the customer to get an understanding of the pain points affecting the customer. As I stated earlier in the book, Lean Six Sigma is a customer-centric methodology, so *try not to lose sight of who you are working for.* These voices of the customer need to be translated into CTQ for process improvement.

Once you believe you have properly listened to the voice of the customer, you will then form your project team from the key stakeholders affected by it. The team roles, like everything else at this stage, should be very clearly defined. As you should have picked up, clarity and definition is a key component of a Lean Six Sigma project–the definition of roles and objectives and so on will be instrumental to the extent of the improvements that the project drives through.

The next chapter will discuss the second stage of DMAIC, that is, Measure, which should set you further on the path to improvement and results!

Quiz

Refresh your memory and check that your understanding of the Define stage is up to scratch by answering these quick questions:

1. A project team should ideally have:
   a. Six to seven team members
   b. Representation from all key stakeholders
   c. Both a and b
   d. None of the above

2. A project charter helps to prevent which of the following in order to enhance the stakeholder buy-in to the project?
   a. Goals that are non specific and abstract
   b. Unclear accountability
   c. Lack of resources
   d. All of the above

3. A team goes through the following sequence:
    a. Forming, norming, storming, performing
    b. Norming, forming, performing, storming
    c. Forming, storming, norming, performing
    d. Storming, forming, norming, performing

4. Conversion of a VOC into a CTQ involves:
    a. Identifying customer, capturing VOC, identifying key issue, create CTQ
    b. Capturing VOC, identifying customer, creating CTQ, identifying key issue
    c. Identifying key issue, capturing VOC, identifying customer, creating CTQ
    d. Creating CTQ, identifying key issue, capturing VOC, identifying customer

5. A project has been going well until the solutions were supposed to be implemented. One of the key stakeholders who is going to be affected by the implemented solution has started raising objections to the proposed solution. This is due to:
    a. The stakeholder is afraid of the change and hence unwilling to implement the solution
    b. The stakeholder not being identified correctly at the start of the project
    c. The intended response of the stakeholder was not mapped correctly and now the sponsor should immediately meet them and bring them on board
    d. Both B and C

6. In a SIPOC, stakeholders are generally:
    a. Customers
    b. Suppliers
    c. Suppliers as well as customers
    d. Not mapped in SIPOC

7. In a SIPOC, a customer is someone:
    a. Who receives an output
    b. End user of a process
    c. Most critical part
    d. Key stakeholder of the process

8. A project charter does not have:
    a. Scope
    b. A problem statement
    c. A control plan
    d. A business case

9. A project sponsor is the one who:
   a. Is generally someone from senior management
   b. Helps clear roadblocks faced by the project team
   c. Both A and B
   d. None of the above

10. In a SIPOC, inputs can be:
   a. Data
   b. Output from other processes
   c. Suppliers' products
   d. All the above

Answers: 1 – C, 2 – D, 3 – C, 4 – A, 5 – D, 6 – C, 7 – A, 8 – C, 9 – C, 10 - D

4

Measure (Day 12-17)

This chapter describes the second stage of the DMAIC methodology—**Measure**. Measure is the next logical step of improvement. It tells us about the current performance level of the process that we intend to improve. This chapter will describe the deliverables of the **Measure** stage along with the tools and techniques to achieve them. At the end of the chapter, we will see the application of this stage to our case study.

Key deliverables

In Lewis Carroll's *Alice in Wonderland*, a fascinating conversation takes place between Alice and the Cheshire Cat:

Alice: Would you tell me, please, which way I ought to go from here?

Cheshire Cat: That depends a good deal on where you want to get to.

Alice: I don't much care where.

Cheshire Cat: Then it doesn't matter which way you go.

Alice: so long as I get *somewhere*.

The project charter in the Define stage helped us to create a roadmap of where we want to go. However, any roadmap is of hardly any use unless we know where we are beginning the journey from. The Measure stage establishes exactly that: the current, as is state of the process that we want to improve. It helps us to establish the current baseline of the process under improvement.

The key deliverables of Measure are:

> Identifying key measures
> A data collection plan
> Measurement system analysis
> A detailed process map
> A Baseline performance measurement or process capability measurement

Let's explore these deliverables in detail.

Identifying key measures (day 12)

The first step in the Measure stage is to define the key performance measures. These performance measures need to be defined *from the customer's perspective.*

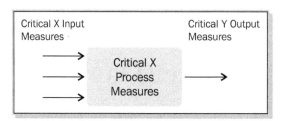

There are three types of measures:

> ➤ **Input measures**: These are measures related to and describing the input into a process. These are the independent variables that constitute some of the Xs that were introduced as part of the equation $Y=f(X)$ in the first chapter. These Xs can be the predictors of process and output measures.

> ➤ **Process measures**: These are measures related to individual steps in the process and/or the overall process. These are also independent variables and constitute some of the Xs as part of the equation $Y=f(X)$. Hence, they can be predictors of output measures. Process measures relate to the effectiveness and efficiency of the resources necessary to transform inputs into outputs. **Effectiveness** refers to how well the output of a process meets the requirements of the customer. In other words it is an outside-in (from the customer's point of view) view of the process and is a measure of customer satisfaction. **Efficiency** refers to the quantity of resources or inputs used to achieve an output. It is an inside-out (from the organization's point of view) view and has an impact on the profitability of the organization.

> ➤ **Output measures**: These are the measures related to the output of the process. These are customer CTQ attributes and the Y part of the equation $Y=f(X)$. These are dependent or response variables.

To help you understand these measures, let's look at an everyday example:

An obese man wants to shed his weight as advised by his physician. In this case, weight is the output measure or Y that the man wishes to act upon. If we look closely at the process of gaining weight, there are certain inputs that affect weight, for example, kind of food, lifestyle, and so on. These are the input or X. Process measures, X, could be for example, calorie intake, calories burned, number of steps walked per day, and so on.

At this stage, the process and input measures are *potential Xs*. Further systematic analysis during the Analyze phase would filter this list of potential critical Xs to the actual critical Xs. As a –rule of thumb, we can work toward identifying three to four measures for each of the input, process, and output measures.

Data collection plan (day 12-14)

After the key measures have been identified, the next step is to prepare a good data collection plan. The data collection plan is a three-step process:

> ➤ Clarify the objectives of data collection
>
> ➤ Develop operational definitions and procedures
>
> ➤ Collect data

Let's look at these steps in detail.

Clarification of objectives

Before you start collecting data, it is important to clarify the objectives behind the data collection. Without this, you may not be able to collect the right data relevant to the project. This involves asking questions such as:

> ➤ Why are we collecting data?
>
> ➤ What data needs to be collected?
>
> ➤ How will this data help?
>
> ➤ What should we do with the data once it has been collected?

Without this clarity, at best data will be meaningless; at worst it could even be misleading.

Developing operational definitions and procedures

This involves defining what is going to be evaluated, how a value will be assigned to what is going to be measured, and how the data will be collected and recorded. There are certain criteria that are essential for a good operational definition:

> ➤ A good operational definition should be clear, specific, and precise
>
> ➤ A good operational definition should ensure that every user (the people who use these measures and definitions) has the same understanding
>
> ➤ A good operational definition states how it will be measured
>
> ➤ A good operational definition is relevant to the customer

Edward Deming described operational definition as a specific thing "that people can do business with....It must be communicable, with the same meaning to vendor as to purchaser, the same meaning yesterday and today."

Make a note

Example of an operational definition

How do we define on-time departure for an airline? One possible example could be: an on-time departure is one in which the door to the Jet way is closed within 5 minutes of the scheduled departure. Airport control provides the time for closure; scheduled departure time is provided by the airport system.

For each flight, the gate supervisor will note the time the Jet way is closed and determine whether each flight left within 5 minutes of the scheduled departure time.

Data that is being measured can be categorized as **continuous** or **discrete**.

➤ **Continuous data**, sometimes called variable data, is based on a continuum or a scale and can be infinitely divided. It may be split, for example, according to length, height, weight, time, temperature, and speed.

➤ **Discrete data**, which is sometimes called attribute data, cannot be infinitely divided and is based on counts, classes, or categories such as Yes-No, Pass-fail, Male-female, proportions, 5-point survey scale, and Defects.

The following table represents the two types of data visually:

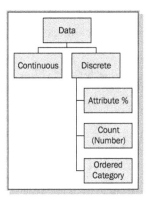

Continuous data is preferred over discrete data because it provides more information. Unlike discrete data, it can be graphed and represented as a time chart. However, continuous data takes more effort and time to capture compared to discrete data.

Collect data

Once we are fairly clear about the operational definitions, we are now ready to collect the data. Data collection is one of the most time-consuming and difficult tasks in a Lean Six Sigma project. One needs to strike a balance between too much and too little data. Usually, Black Belts can guide the team on the optimal amount of data required.

A critical part of a data collection exercise is the design of data collection forms. A very simple but effective data collection form is a **check sheet**.

Check sheets are primarily used to collect new data when historic data is not available. They are used to collect data in real time and at the location where the data is being generated. They can be used to capture quantitative as well as qualitative data. A typical check sheet defines different attributes and displays "checks" or tally marks to show the counts against these attributes. Check sheets can be used for the following tasks:

➤ To quantify Defects by type

➤ To quantify defects by location

➤ To quantify defects by cause

➤ To keep a track of the progress of activities in a project

➤ To check the shape of the probability distribution of a process (we will discuss probability distribution in detail in a subsequent section)

An example of a check sheet is given in the following table. Whenever an attribute is observed, a tally is marked against it. At the end these tally marks are counted, which is shown in the **Total** column.

Title : Defects in Invoices			
Collector	Cathy Peters	Date of collection	5/25/2012
Instructions: Please use tally marks against the attribute in an invoice a defect is observed			
Attribute	Tally		Total
Spelling mistake	⊞⊞ ⊞⊞ ⊞⊞ II		17
Incomplete address	⊞⊞ ⊞⊞ IIII		14
Incorrect amount	⊞⊞ IIII		9
Tax terms not clear	IIII		4
Total			44

The next crucial step in data collection is the **sampling plan**.

Sampling refers to the collection of a small part of an entire data set, called the **"population"**, which is used to infer the attributes of the population. This is done because the collection and use of large data can be cumbersome and uneconomical. The sampling plan involves the following:

➤ *Definition of the target population.* The target population is basically the population from which the samples will be drawn. This target population needs to be relevant to the process being improved. The selection of a target population involves consideration of the time frame from which the historical data is collected. A guideline for this could be that only data that provides information about the current state of the process should be collected. Active data may be collected when there is no historical data available. *Selection of a sampling methodology.* When selecting a sampling methodology, one must consider:

  ➤ The sample drawn should be **representative** of the population, meaning all variations within a particular population—this could be shift times, experience, and so on, -are accounted for in the sample.

  ➤ Sampling error (bias) is minimal.

Make a note

A **representative** sample provides equal opportunity of selection to all the different sections and segments that may be part of the population. A sampling error or bias is due to systematic errors that may creep into the sampling plan or strategy. It is important to be mindful of these errors or this bias. Some examples of bias are **response bias**, which refers to some sections not responding to the surveys, hence not getting adequate representation; **convenience sampling bias**, which refers to choosing a sample based on ease and convenience, thus leaving out some sections of the population; **environmental bias**, which refers to a bias due to a change in conditions from the time the sample was drawn to the time when the conclusions are being drawn from the sample; and **measurement system bias**, which refers to errors due to the process of measurement.

The design of your sampling strategy depends upon how you look at the data. The **process data** involves observing the process as it takes place. The **population data** on the other hand requires you to look at the output without worrying about the inherent process.

In other words, the **process approach** involves assessing the stability of the population over time. For example, if I stand in front of the machine that is producing units and observe the process, and while observing the process I pick up samples at some predefined frequency, this would be the process approach. The **population approach**, meanwhile, makes probability statements about the population based on the sample. For example, if I just stand at the end of the process and randomly pick up samples from the basket that stores the output of the process, this would be the population approach; while the former allows you to view a process in real time, the latter lets you see retrospectively, giving you a historical view.

The various sampling strategies for the two approaches are described in the following table:

Approach	Sampling strategy	Description	Illustration
Population	Simple random sampling	Units are drawn from the population randomly so that each unit has an equal chance of being picked up	
Population	Stratified random sampling	Samples representing various groups or strata or sections are randomly picked up from the population in proportion to the relative size of these groups or strata	
Process	Systematic sampling	Samples are picked up based on some pattern, for example, every 4th unit	
Process	Rational sub-group sampling	A sub-group sample size of say 3-4 units are picked up as per a fixed pattern, for example, 3-4 consecutive units every hour	

Evaluation of sample size

The next step involves drawing out the sample from the population. The size of the sample is dependent on:

➤ Acceptable **measurement error**, E
➤ Variability of the process data
➤ Confidence level

A measurement error is also called the **margin of error** and is written as an interval called the **confidence interval**. This refers to how precise the estimated value is with respect to the true value and is written as, for example, +/- 3 percent of the true value. Since a sample characteristic is an estimate of the population characteristic, there will always be a likelihood of the former being different from the true value of the characteristic. This difference is defined as the margin of error. The measurement of error is generally between 2-9 percent. The higher the criticality of the process, the lower the value of this measurement error.

Make a note

For normal processes, the value of the confidence interval is generally taken as 5 percent.

The confidence level is a percentage related to the probability of accuracy of the sample measure in relation to the wider population of a data set. A confidence level of 95 percent implies that 95 times out of 100, the sample measure will be within the stated confidence interval of the true population measure. Generally, this confidence level is depicted by **Z, standardized score**. An abridged table for *Z* values for various confidence levels is provided in the text later. A complete Z table explanation is available in any standard statistics textbook.

Make a note

Generally, a confidence level of 95 percent is used for normal processes. The Z value for 95 percent confidence level is 1.96.

Depending upon the type of data, the following table gives the formula for the sample size:

Type of data	Sample size formula
Continuous	$n=(Z*S\,/E)^2$ where n=sample size Z=standardized score for a confidence level S=standard deviation E=acceptable measurement error
Discrete	$n=(Z/E)^{2}*\,p(1\text{-}p)]$ where n=sample size E= acceptable measurement error Z= standardized score for a confidence level P=estimated proportion of correct observations

Make a note

The sample size is independent of the population size.

The two following examples show you how to use the previous formula to calculate the required sample size for continuous and discrete data.

Make a note

Example 1: What is the sample size required to determine the mean time to process an insurance claim with a confidence level of 95 percent when the standard deviation is estimated at 16 minutes and the acceptable measurement error is +/-5 percent?

Answer: The data is continuous. Hence, n=(ZS/E)² . Here, Z=1.96, Standard deviation(S)=16 and Margin of error (E)=5

n= [(1.96)(16)/5]²=39.33 ~ 40 (rounded to the next integer)

Example 2: What is the sample size to estimate the proportion of defective components with a 95 percent confidence level and an acceptable measurement error of +/-5 percent? Historical data shows the proportion of defective data as 20 percent.

Answer: The proportion of defective data is discrete data. Hence, n=[Z/ E]²*p(1-p). Here, Z=1.96, E = .05, p=0.20

n= [1.96/.05]²(0.20)(0.80) = 246 (rounded to the next integer)

The following table provides some –rules of thumb for the minimum sample size:

Tool Or Statistic	Minimum Sample Size
Average	5-10
Standard Deviation	25-30
Proportion Defective (P)	100 And nP ≥ 5
Histogram Or Pareto Chart	50
Scatter Diagram	25
Control Chart	20

Since we now know how to calculate sample size, let's explore the possible errors that there may be in the way we measure the data, and how we can minimize these errors.

Measurement system analysis (day 15)

We introduced the concept of bias in the previous section. **Measurement system analysis (MSA)** enables you to identify the specific biases that are caused by the system of measurement itself. Total process variation typically comprises variations from two sources— *variation inherent in the process* and *variation due to measurement*. Mathematically, this may be represented as:

$\sigma^2 total = \sigma^2 process + \sigma^2 measurement$

The measurement system needs to be analyzed for the following:

Parameter	Definition
Accuracy	Difference in the average measurement compared to a standard
Repeatability	Variation in measurements when the same person repeats the measurement with the same measuring equipment
Reproducibility	Variation in measurement when two or more people take measurements with the same measuring equipment
Stability	Variation in the measurement over an extended period of time when measurements are done by the same person with the same equipment
Linearity	Consistency of the measurement system across the entire range of the measurement system

Gage R&R

Gage R&R is one of the primary tools to estimate the variance in the measurements. As described in the previous table, it basically calculates repeatability and reproducibility. This combined value can then be used as an indication of the variation due to the measurement system. Mathematically, Gage R&R is represented as:

percent R&R = (σ Measurement system / σ Total) X 100

σ Measurement system = ($\sigma2$ repeatability + $\sigma2$ reproducibility)1/2

The discrimination ratio refers to the number of distinct categories or classes that the measurement equipment can discern. A value of 2, for example, implies that the measurement system can be used only for attribute analysis where parts can be categorized into one group or the other. This can also be seen as the measure of the **resolution** of the measuring equipment. Resolution refers to the smallest change in a measured value that the measuring equipment can detect. For example, a digital stopwatch has two digits beyond the seconds so it divides time into hundredths of a second. Since it can give us readings up to 1/100th of a second, its resolution is 1/100 second. The higher the discrimination ratio, the greater the resolution of the measurement system.

Make a note

A good measurement system should have a Gage R&R value below 10percent and a discrimination ratio of 4 and above.

We need to take corrective steps to ensure that these conditions are met before embarking on the actual measurement.

Manual calculation of Gage R&R is very cumbersome. These calculations can be easily done by some of the standard statistical software such as Minitab, SPSS, JMP, and so on available on the market.

Data representation (day 15)

The data that we collected in the previous steps needs to be represented in a meaningful way for an effective analysis. This depends on the following factors:

➤ **Type of data**.

➤ **Variation over a period of time**: The entire data for a period is collected and the variation in the data is studied. The different time intervals for this period are irrelevant from this perspective (population data).

➤ **Variation with time**: This perspective involves looking at the data at different time intervals over a certain period (process data).

The following table provides a summary of the ways the different types of data can be represented.

Type Of Data	Variation over a period of time	Variation with Time
Discrete	■ Pareto Diagram ■ Bar Charts ■ Pie Charts	■ Run Charts ■ Control Charts p-Chart c-Chart u-Chart Individual Measurement
Continuous	■ Histograms/Frequency Diagrams ■ Box Plots ■ Multi-Vari Charts	■ Run Charts ■ Control Charts Individual Measurement X-R Chart

Let's take a look at some of these tools.

Pareto diagram

A Pareto diagram is a type of vertical bar chart that ranks related measures in a descending order of their occurrence. It uses the **Pareto principle**, also known as the 80/20 rule: roughly 80percent of the effects are caused by 20percent of causes. It helps us to identify the really important factors that make a difference to the results of the process.

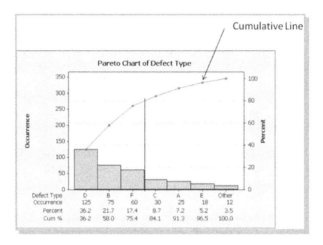

The horizontal axis displays the factors being considered in descending order of occurrence. The vertical axis on the left side represents the frequency of occurrence of these factors, while the right axis represents the cumulative percentage for these occurrences. If we drop a perpendicular from the cumulative line, say at a point corresponding to 80 percent on the cumulative percentage axis, to the horizontal axis, all the factors to the left of this perpendicular line will tell us the factors that correspond to 80 percent of the defects. As you can see in the previous figure, three types—D, B, and F—account for 80 percent of the defective units.

Bar chart

A bar chart is a chart with rectangular bars whose lengths are in proportion to the value they represent. These bars can be arranged vertically or horizontally and provide a simple comparison of the various factors or categories. For example, a bar chart to show the comparison of sales in different months is shown as follows:

Pie chart

A pie chart is a circular chart that shows different sectors whose arc lengths represent the numerical proportion of various categories. This can help us identify in a graphical form which of the factors or segments constitutes a bigger proportion of the whole. This helps us prioritize and focus on the vital few rather than the unimportant many. An example of a pie chart is shown as follows:

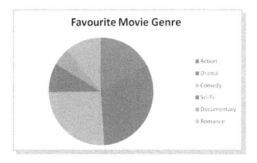

Histogram

Histograms are graphical representations of data distributions. They are an estimate of probability distribution of the continuous variable. They represent the tabulated frequencies with the help of adjacent rectangles whose area is equal to the frequency of the observation. An example of a histogram that shows the distribution of days taken to resolve an issue by a technical help center is given as follows:

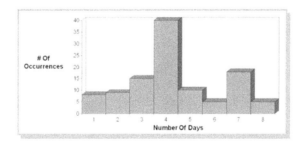

The shape, size, and location of the distribution can provide a lot of useful information about the pattern of variation in the data.

Box plot

A box plot is another graphical summary of a pattern of variations within the data. A typical box plot looks like this:

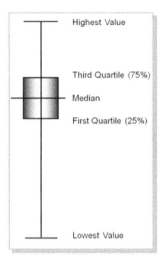

As you can see from the figure, the middle box represents 50percent of data between the first quartile and the third quartile. The horizontal line within the box shows the median value, while the lower and the upper ends of the box represent the first and third quartiles respectively. The width of the box tells us about the variation in the data. *The higher the variation, the wider the box.* Multiple box plots taken together can provide comparisons between different populations without any assumption about the underlying distribution. See the following figure:

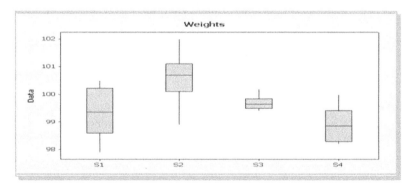

Multi-vari chart

Multi-vari charts are used to analyze variation due to, sample variation, unit-to-unit variation, and time-to-time variation. It is a 2-axis plot with a horizontal axis denoting time and the measured parameter on the vertical axis. Each unit is measured multiple times and these measurements are plotted together. The units constituting a sub-group are plotted from left to right over time. An example of this chart is provided as follows:

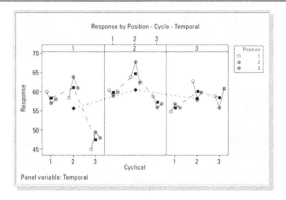

Run chart

A run chart is a time-ordered plot of data and is used to ascertain patterns that can point towards non-random causes of variation. A typical run-chart looks like this:

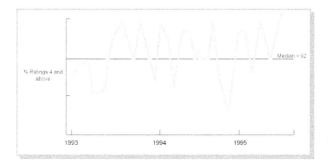

Control chart

Like a run chart, a control chart is also a time-ordered plot but it contains two control limits—Upper and Lower control limits (UCL and LCL) based on the mean and standard variation of the process. It is also used to analyze non-random variations in the process. It is used to verify whether the process is stable and under statistical control. There are a number of different types of control charts, which we will discuss later in more detail in the *Control* stage.

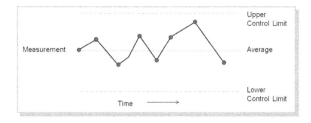

Although the various tools described previously can also be created manually, it is advisable that we use statistical software. Minitab, SAS JMP, Sigma XL, Statgraphics, and SPSS are some of the statistical software packages widely available in the market.

A detailed process map (day 15-16)

Now we have the data, we are now able to observe the process under examination and identify the value adding and non-value adding activities within it that lead to delays and errors.

For this, a detailed process map is drawn up with all the key functions and roles involved in the process. This is called a **cross-functional process map**. This is a tool from Lean methodology. The steps involved in creating a cross-functional process map are:

> ➤ Identify the customer and other participants of the process and list them vertically on the left-hand side.

> ➤ Identify the first and the last step of the process

> ➤ Identify the participant who interacts with the customer and the activity they perform and write the activity against the row of the respective participant

> ➤ Identify the output of this activity and the recipient of this output

> ➤ Keep performing these steps until the process is complete, that is, the final step as listed in step i) is reached

The following is an example of a process diagram:

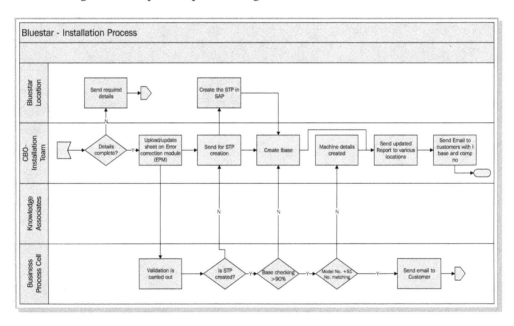

The time taken for each of these activities should also be noted down. There are many automated tools available such as MS Visio, which is an extremely useful tool to produce cross-functional process maps.

Baseline performance measurement (day 16-17)

Now, we are ready to calculate the current performance capability. But before we do that, it would be worthwhile to revise some basic statistics.

Statistics can be of two types: **descriptive** and **inferential**. Descriptive statistics *describe characteristics* about a population or a sample of data. Inferential statistics involves *drawing inferences about the characteristics* of a population from a sample of data. Lean Six Sigma mostly employs inferential statistics.

One of the fundamental concepts in statistics is that of **probability**. Probability is the likelihood that an event or outcome will occur. When these probabilities are plotted against the different values of the event or outcome, we get a **probability distribution**. For example, the likelihood of a head or a tail turning up when we toss a coin is 0.5 each. If we plot the outcomes of the toss when the coin has been tossed a large number of times, we get the probability distribution curve for the toss of the coin. There are different types of probability distribution curves.

Lean Six Sigma is interested mostly in **normal distribution**, shown as follows:

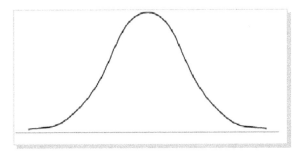

Make a note

Normal distribution is a probability distribution where the most frequently occurring value is in the middle and other probabilities tail off symmetrically in both directions from this middle value.

Also known as a **normal curve**, the characteristics of normal distribution are as follows:

> ➤ Theoretically, the curve does not reach zero.

> ➤ The curve is symmetrical on both the sides of the most frequently occurring value.

> ➤ It indicates random or chance variation. This is very significant because Six Sigma uses the assumption of random variation.

> ➤ The peak of the curve represents the center of the process.

> ➤ The area under the curve represents 100percent of the outcome from the process.

If we drop perpendiculars to the x axis of this curve at various integer multiples of the standard deviation on both sides of the center, we get an indication of the percentage of values lying within the area enclosed by the two lines. This curve can be divided into segments as follows:

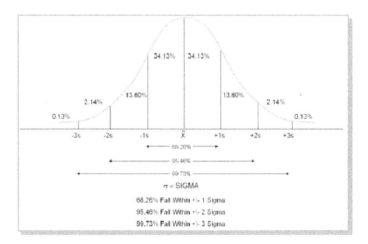

Most data distributions can be characterized by two different measures:

➤ Central tendency, which measures using the mean, mode, and median

➤ Dispersion, which can be measured using range and standard deviation

The following table summarizes the different measures associated with the central tendency and dispersion:

#	Parameter	Description	Formula
1	Mean	Most likely or expected value in the sample	$$\bar{x} = \frac{1}{n}\sum_{i=1}^{n} x$$ Insert image 0340IM_04_17.png n = sample size x = observed value
2	Mode	Most frequently occurring value in the sample	--
3	Median	The central value in the sample	The values are arranged in ascending order. For an even n, the median is the average of the middle two values. For an odd n, the median is the middle value.
4	Range	The difference between the highest and the lowest values	Highest value – Lowest value.
5	Standard deviation	Average distance a given value is from the mean of the sample	$$s = \sqrt{\frac{1}{n-1}\sum_{i=1}^{n}(x-\bar{x})^2}$$ Insert image 0340IM_04_18.png n = sample size x = observed value $\bar{x}$ = mean value

Standard normal distribution is a special type of normal distribution curve with mean and standard deviation of 0 and 1 respectively. A normal distribution needs to be converted into a standard normal distribution to make use of the standard normal table (described later in this chapter). This standard table comes in handy while calculating baseline performance data for continuous data. Any normal distribution can be transformed into a standard normal distribution by using the following formula:

$Z = (X - \mu)/\sigma$

Where:

➤ X = variable of interest from the original normal distribution

➤ μ = the mean of the original normal distribution

➤ σ = the standard deviation of the original normal distribution

The Z value indicates the number of standard deviations apart from the mean of a particular X.

Now, let's return our focus to the calculation of baseline performance capability. Depending on discrete and continuous data, there are two ways of calculating baseline performance capability. The method to calculate the current performance baseline is described in the following sections.

For discrete data

Defects per million opportunities (DPMO) is one of the most widely used methods to calculate the current performance of a process. This measures the number of defects generated within one million opportunities for them to occur. This DPMO can then be converted into a sigma value using a standard table.

The formula for DPMO is as follows:

$DPMO = [D / (N * O)]*100000$

Where:

➤ D = Number of defects. A defect is an instance when customer requirement is not met.

➤ N = Number of units. A unit is defined as the product or transaction processed.

➤ O = Defect opportunity per unit. Opportunity is defined as an event that can be measured and has a likelihood of not meeting customer's requirement.

Example: 500 invoices are processed. Each invoice could result in a defect in three ways – being late, wrong amount, and wrong address. There were 57 errors across these 500 voices. What is the sigma level of the process?

DPMO = [D / (N * O)]*1,000,000

   = [57/500*3]*1000000= 38000

Sigma level = 3.3 (nearest sigma value closest to 38,000 in the following table.)

The following table gives the various sigma values against the respective DPMO. It also provides yield, which is the measure of non-defects and is calculated as (100-percent defects).

Sigma	Yield (percent)	DPMO	Sigma	Yield (percent)	DPMO
1	30.23	697672	3.6	98.21	17865
1.1	33.99	660083	3.7	98.61	13903
1.2	37.86	621378	3.8	98.93	10724
1.3	41.82	581815	3.9	99.18	8198
1.4	45.84	541694	4	99.379	6210
1.5	49.86	501350	4.1	99.534	4661
1.6	53.89	461140	4.2	99.653	3467

Sigma	Yield (percent)	DPMO	Sigma	Yield (percent)	DPMO
1.7	57.86	421428	4.3	99.745	2555
1.8	61.75	382572	4.4	99.813	1866
1.9	65.51	344915	4.5	99.865	1350
2	69.12	308770	4.6	99.903	968
2.1	72.56	274412	4.7	99.931	687
2.2	75.80	242071	4.8	99.952	483
2.3	78.80	211928	4.9	99.966	337
2.4	81.59	184108	5	99.9767	233
2.5	84.13	158687	5.1	99.9841	159
2.6	86.43	135687	5.2	99.9892	108
2.7	88.49	115083	5.3	99.9928	72
2.8	90.32	96809	5.4	99.9952	48
2.9	91.92	80762	5.5	99.9968	32
3	93.32	66811	5.6	99.9979	21
3.1	94.52	54801	5.7	99.9987	13
3.2	95.54	44567	5.8	99.9991	9
3.3	96.41	35931	5.9	99.9995	5
3.4	97.13	28717	6	99.99966	3.4
3.5	97.73	22750			

Make a note

A Six Sigma process generates 3.4 defects per million opportunities.

For continuous data

For continuous data, we use standard normal distribution. The steps are as follows:

1. Draw a standard normal curve and label the mean, upper specification limit (USL), and lower specification limit (LSL) and integer multiples of standard deviation. The USL and LSL limits refer to the highest and the lowest values of a parameter that a customer is going to accept. Anything that does not fall within these limits is a defect.

2. Calculate the area beyond USL using the following formula:

   ➤ $Z^1 = (USL - mean) / \sigma$

3. Look up the value corresponding to Z^1 in the normal table (given later in this section).

4. Calculate Area^1= 1-[value obtained in (3)].

5. Calculate the area beyond LSL using the following formula:

   ➢ Z^2= (LSL - mean) / σ

6. Look up the value corresponding to Z2 in the normal table (given later in this section).

7. Calculate Area^2= value obtained in (vi).

8. Determine the Total area = Area^1+ Area^2.

9. Calculate percent Yield = (1 – Total area) * 100.

10. Look up the sigma value in the following sigma table (abridged). Please refer any standard statistics textbook for the complete table.

				Decimal						
	0.0	0.1	0.2	0.3	0.4	0.5	0.6	0.7	0.8	0.9
-4	0.000032	0.000021	0.000013	0.000009	0.000005	0.000003	0.000002	0.000001	0.000001	0.000000
-3	0.001350	0.000968	0.000687	0.000483	0.000337	0.000233	0.000159	0.000108	0.000072	0.000048
-2	0.022750	0.017864	0.013903	0.010724	0.008198	0.006210	0.004661	0.003467	0.002555	0.001866
-1	0.158655	0.135666	0.115070	0.096801	0.080757	0.066807	0.054799	0.044565	0.035930	0.028716
Whole -0	0.500000	0.460172	0.420740	0.382089	0.344578	0.308538	0.274253	0.241964	0.211855	0.184060
Number 0	0.500000	0.539828	0.579260	0.617911	0.655422	0.691462	0.725747	0.758036	0.788145	0.815940
1	0.841345	0.864334	0.884930	0.903199	0.919243	0.933193	0.945201	0.955435	0.964070	0.971284
2	0.977250	0.982136	0.986097	0.989276	0.991802	0.993790	0.995339	0.996533	0.997445	0.998134
3	0.998650	0.999032	0.999313	0.999517	0.999663	0.999767	0.999841	0.999892	0.999928	0.999952
4	0.999968	0.999979	0.999987	0.999991	0.999995	0.999997	0.999998	0.999999	0.999999	1.000000

If there is only one specification limit (USL or LSL), the corresponding steps may be ignored. The following example will further clarify the calculation:

Make a note

Example: In a tube manufacturing process, tube diameter has USL and LSL as 3 mm and 2.6 mm respectively. The mean observed is 2.8 mm and standard deviation is 0.05 mm. What is the sigma level of this process?

Answer:

Z1 = (USL – mean) / σ = (3 – 2.8) / 0.05 = 4

Z1 value as per normal table = 0.999968

Area1 = (1- 0.999968) = 0.000032

Z2 = (LSL- mean) / σ = (2.6 – 2.8) / 0.05 = - 4

Z2 value as per normal table = 0.000032

Area2=0.000032

Total Area = Area1+Area2=0.000032+0.000032 = 0.000064

percent Yield = (1- Total area) * 100 = (1- 0.000064)*100 = 99.9936

Sigma value (from the previous sigma table) = 5.3

For a more detailed discussion on the statistical concepts and tools covered in this chapter and the chapters that follow, please refer to some standard statistics textbooks, for example, *Statistics for Management, Richard Levin and David Rubin, Applied Statistics and Probability for Engineers, D.C. Montgomery and G C Runger, Statistics for Business and Economics, H Kohler,* and *Statistics for Dummies, Deborah J Rumsey.*

This concludes the Measure stage. We now have the data at our disposal that can be used during the Analyze stage. We also validated the measurement system. We created a detailed cross-functional process map and evaluated the current performance baseline. We are now ready to move to the next stage. In the real world, the Measure and Analyze stages are more or less simultaneous stages. Analysis can start as we collect the data. We will cover the analysis stage in the next chapter.

The following section describes a continuation of the case study we have been looking at in previous chapters. This will enable you to see how the measure stage is executed, but also how it fits into the broader picture of your Lean Six Sigma initiative.

Case study – Measure

The Measure stage for the case study will be discussed in the following section.

The team discussed the various Project *Y*s and the corresponding operational definitions and measurement plans. The Project *Y*s were as follows:

> ➤ Customer satisfaction as the primary Y to be measured through a monthly industry standard survey as well as an internal mechanism to collect ratings for a sample set of customers every week

> ➤ Cost per call as the secondary Y to be measured using the time taken to service a call and standard unit cost received from Finance and Accounts department

> ➤ Issue resolution time, wait time, hold time, call back, days to resolution, transfers, and so on collected through call management software

> ➤ The performance standards for each of the above Ys were also arrived at using current as well as the benchmark data.

> ➤ The primary Y was thought to be related to the *X*s such as wait time, hold time, resolution time, average handling time, call backs, days to resolution, and transfers. Similarly the cost per call was dependent on call volume, average handling time, hold time, call backs, and transfers.

> ➤ An MSA study on the measurement systems revealed the measurement system to be acceptable with Gage R&R as 10percent and the discrimination ratio as 4.

The data was collected in the following format:

Call	Week	Day	Staffing	Volumes	Type of call	Transfers	Wait Time	Resolution Time	Hold Time	Average Handle Time	Call back	Days to resolution	Support Cost $
1	1	Mon	35	250	Hardware	5	7.2	25.4	5.5	38.1	2	5	35.6
2	1	Mon	35	250	Hardware	2	6.3	20.2	4.8	31.3	1	6	30.2
3	1	Mon	35	250	Software	0	8.5	16.4	4.5	29.4	0	1	28.3
4	1	Mon	35	250	Internet	1	3.1	7.5	2	12.6	1	2	8.5
1300	2	Wed	38	275	Gen Query	0	2.1	4.8	0.5	7.4	0	0	8
1301	2	Wed	38	275	software	2	5.7	20.6	5.6	31.9	0	1	31.3
1302	2	Wed	38	275	Internet	1	3.4	8.5	1.2	13.1	1	1	9.1
2500	3	Tue	40	300	Hardware	3	3.5	26.8	5.8	36.1	2	2	33.5
2501	3	Tue	40	300	Hardware	4	2.6	13.2	2.4	18.2	0	1	12.7
3800	4	Mon	35	258	Internet	1	4.2	7.8	1.5	13.5	1	1	10.2
3801	4	Mon	35	258	Gen Query	0	3.2	2.5	0	5.7	0	0	6.3
4500	5	Thu	33	243	Gen Query	1	3.8	4.6	1.2	9.6	0	0	7.4

Summary

Measure is a stage that allows us to get to grips with the gap between the target and actual performance—precisely what Six Sigma aims to tackle. The stage involves a comprehensive data collection plan with a clear definition of what data needs to be collected, for what duration, and how it should be reported. This ensures that the data is both uniform and as extensive as possible. Before data gets collected, it is also essential that we ensure that the measurement system that we are using is also correct, stable, and without significant variation. The data collected can be represented in various ways depending on the type of data and the perspective for the process and the data. A detailed cross-functional process map helps to graphically define the process and the participants along with the time taken for each of the activities of the process. This will help during the Analyze stage to identify value-adding and non-value adding steps. Towards the end, we will calculate the current process performance baseline to know the current state of the process. This helps in setting up the target sigma level that we would like to reach for the process with the Lean Six Sigma project.

The stage is now set to analyze the data being covered in the next chapter. Analysis will help to reduce numerous potential Xs to few actual Xs that impact the output.

Quiz

1. Measurement error:

    a. A. Does not matter

    b. B. Is estimated by MSA studies

    c. C. Is due to the incompetence of the operator

    d. D. None of the above

2. Measurement systems analysis is needed because:

    a. A. Inaccurate measurements may lead to erroneous analysis

    b. B. Calibration cannot eliminate all measurement errors

    c. C. Different personnel making a measurement using the same equipment may report different values

    d. D. All of the above

3. With respect to the equation Y=f(x):

    a. A. Output measures are represented by Y

    b. B. Input measures are related to the inputs to a process

    c. C. Input measures are independent variables that constitute some Xs

    d. D. Process measures are related to the steps in the process and can be predictors for the Y

    e. E. All of the above

4. An operational definition is required:
   a. To remove ambiguity and ensure everyone has the same understanding
   b. To provide a clear way to measure a characteristic
   c. To assist data collection and analysis
   d. All of the above

5. A good sampling plan must ensure that:
   a. The sample drawn is representative of the population
   b. There is no systematic bias
   c. The samples are drawn as per the convenience of the user
   d. All of the above
   e. Only A and B

6. For a measurement system to be acceptable:
   a. Gage R&R should be less than 15percent
   b. The discrimination ratio should be more than 4
   c. Only A
   d. Only B
   e. Both A and B

7. A 90 percent confidence interval for the mean is from 12.675 to 15.285. This means that:
   a. There is 90 percent probability that the true mean lies between 12.675 and 15.285
   b. 90 percent of all values in the population lie between 12.675 and 15.285
   c. 90 percent of all the sample values in the population lie between 12.675 and 15.285
   d. None of the above

8. A standard normal distribution:
   a. Has a mean of 0 and a standard deviation of 1
   b. Is used to convert any normal distribution by using transformation equation
      $Z = (X - \mu)/\sigma$
   c. Makes use of a normal table more easily
   d. All of the above

9. A car-making company wants to determine its current sigma level. It found that a car can have 150 kinds of defects. It analyzed 3,500 cars that it manufactured last year and found there were 375 defects observed in all. What is the DPMO, yield, and sigma level?

   a. DPMO = 714.3, yield = 99.93, Sigma= 4.1

   b. DPMO = 7143, yield = 99.29, Sigma = 4.1

   c. DPMO = 714.3, Yield = 99.93, Sigma = 4.7

   d. DPMO = 71.43, Yield = 99.993, Sigma = 5.3

10. Which of these statements are true for a normal curve?

   a. It is symmetrical on both the sides of most frequently occurring value

   b. It indicates non-random variation in the process

   c. The area under the curve represents 100percent of values in the process

   d. A and C

   e. Only B

Answers:

11. B
12. D
13. E
14. D
15. E
16. D
17. A
18. D
19. C
20. E

>5

Analyze (Day 14-19)

This chapter describes the third stage, analyze. It is at this stage that we begin to look at the collected data to identify the root causes that contribute certain effects to the final outcome of the process. The objective is to identify and prioritize all the possible causes of variation so that actions can be taken to improve the process. This chapter will describe the core objectives of the analyze stage along with the tools and techniques to achieve these objectives. At the end of the chapter, we will see the application of this stage to our case study.

Key deliverables

The project charter in the define stage helped us to create a roadmap of where we want to go. The measure stage established the current, as-is state of the process that we want to improve. The next stage, analyze, scrutinizes the potential factors collected in the measure stage to identify actual factors that significantly impact the outcome and to prioritize them. Although, for the convenience of discussion, we discuss measure and analyze separately, in real life, they may overlap and may go almost hand-in-hand.

The key deliverables of the analyze stage are:

1. Identification and prioritization of root causes
2. Hypothesis testing

Let's explore these deliverables in some more detail.

Identification and prioritization of root causes (day 14-17)

The first step in the analyze stage is to identify the root causes.

A root cause is the condition or set of conditions that contribute to the creation of problems within a specific process. The elimination or reengineering of the root cause is what will drive improvement, and this is what the objective of Lean Six Sigma is. Just like the roots of a tree, the root cause of a problem may not be visible - data may need to be "shoveled" to unearth it.

There are different ways to identify the root cause(s):

1. Cause and effect diagram
2. Data analysis
3. Process analysis

Cause-and-effect diagram (day 14)

Also known as a fish-bone or Ishikawa diagram, named after its inventor Kauro Ishikawa, a cause and effect diagram provides a graphical representation of contributing causes.

The causes are categorized into broad categories. Some of these categories in a manufacturing setup may include people, material, Mother Nature or environment, method, machinery, measurement, and so on. These categories can be customized according to the needs of the process. These causes can be obtained through brainstorming sessions. Brainstorming refers to a group of people discussing a topic and suggesting various ideas around the topic. We will discuss brainstorming in detail in the improve stage. The effect forms the "head" of the fish.

A typical cause and effect diagram looks like this:

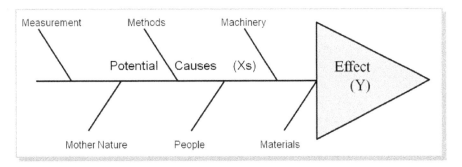

These are the steps to draw an effective cause and effect diagram:

1. Identify the problem or the effect: Write the effect or the problem at the extreme right-hand side of the paper in a triangle and draw a horizontal line from the triangle as shown previously. Only one effect or problem should be written for a diagram.

2. Identify the major primary factors contributing to the effect: The suggested categories in the preceding diagram can be used to begin with. Draw lines above the horizontal line you created in step 1 and label them with these factors. These are the primary factors.

3. Identify possible causes: Brainstorm and identify possible causes under each of these primary factors by asking "why" and show these causes as smaller lines emerging from the lines you created in step 2. Repeat this step for these secondary causes until we have tertiary causes (causes for the secondary causes) and a well branched cause and effect diagram. The causes should be written so that they are specific, concrete, and complete rather than being generic, abstract, and incomplete.

4. Review the diagram to club or group together duplicate causes. Generally, as we go deeper into the process, we find causes converging to 5-7 root causes.

The root causes you discover can be further validated by collecting data.

An example of a well-branched cause and effect diagram with primary, secondary, and tertiary causes is given as follows. You can clearly see how each of the causes falls into their relevant categories and are brought together to feed into the effect. As a result, the cause and effect diagram should really give you a wide and extensive sense of what is causing problems in your processes.

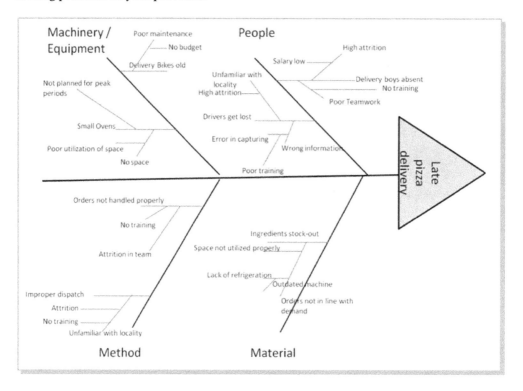

Data analysis (day 14-15)

Some useful analytical tools and techniques were introduced in the previous chapter. The analysis of data collected in the measure stage depends on the type of data collected, discrete or continuous.

Discrete data analysis primarily involves tools such as Pareto charts, pie charts, and bar diagrams. As discussed earlier, Pareto charts tell us about the significant contributors to the outcome. It is also known as "vital-few-trivial-many" or the 80/20 principle, and is a very effective tool that enables us to focus on the vital factors.

Continuous data analysis involves tools such as frequency distribution diagrams, for example histograms and box plots. Histograms can provide a lot of information about the variation and the central tendency of the process. Some of the common shapes of histograms are given in the following table:

Plot	Observe	Analysis	Action
	Symmetric, bell-shaped	If chart shows no special causes, data may come from a stable process.	
	Bi-modal, two humps	Data may come from a combination of two distinct sub-processes within the process e.g. a process where both experienced staff and inexperienced staff participate.	Investigate the two sub—processes separately.
	Asymmetric, long tail	Data may come from a process which is not easily explained with simple mathematical assumptions (like normality).. The data may be concentrated towards higher or lower limits.	Consider transformation and proceed with caution.

Similar to histograms, **box plots** also provide information about the variation and the central tendency of the process. A **multiple box plot** can show comparisons between different elements of the process. For example, the multiple box plot shown in the following screenshot is a comparative study of motor shafts produced by three different lathe machines in a workshop:

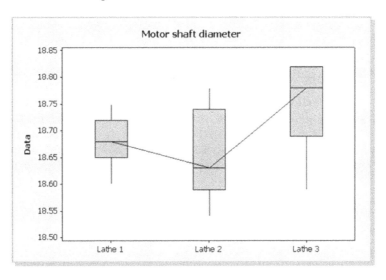

As you can see, there is a wide disparity between the three lathes in terms of variation (displayed by the various widths of the boxes), median values (displayed by the central line within the boxes), and also various inter-quartile values. The screenshot shows that lathe 1 is the most consistent machine of the three machines. The median value of lathe 2 is the lowest among the three machines.

Variation in any process can be due to two types of causes: common causes and special causes. There are usually 6 sources of variation, known as the 6 M's. These 6 M's are man, machine, method, material, measurement, and 'Mother Nature'. The following table describes the two types of causes:

Type	Definition	
Common Cause	No **undue** influence of any or a combination of the 6M's	• Expected • Normal • Random
Special Cause	**Some undue** influence of any or a combination of 6M's	• Unexpected • Not normal • Not random

For example, if I were to plot the time I take to reach my office, the normal fluctuations in the time is attributed to common causes. But suppose there was an accident on the way that held me in the traffic snarl that ensued; there would be a significant jump in the time I take to reach the office. In this case, this fluctuation would be attributed to a special cause, namely traffic due to an accident.

Most of the tools used in Six Sigma assume normality, and hence assume the presence of only common causes of variation. If the data suggests that special causes are present, these should be removed first before moving ahead to the next stages.

A run chart is another effective tool to help you analyze a process in order to identify special causes of variation and eliminate them. It is a line graph of data plotted over time. Observations can reveal trends and patterns in the line graph. It does not have control limits like control charts and can point towards unusual trends and patterns and the possible presence of special causes. The steps involved in creating and analyzing a run chart are:

1. Collect 20 or more data values over time.
2. Plot the data in time order.
3. Draw the median line.

4. Count the 'runs' above and below median. A run is defined as a single point or a series of sequential points where no point is on the other side of the median. Also, while counting runs about the median, omit any points on the median line, and when counting the number of points in a run to determine whether you have a trend or an alternating up and down pattern, omit any points that repeat the preceding value.

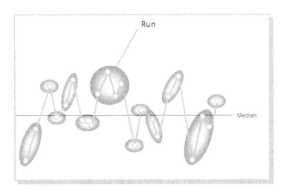

5. Check for signs of special causes using the following chart:

There are special causes if :

Number of Data Points*	You See Fewer Runs Than This	You See More Runs Than This
10	3	8
11	3	9
12	3	10
13	4	10
14	4	11
15	4	12
16	5	12
17	5	13
18	6	13
19	6	14
20	6	15
21	7	15
22	7	16
23	8	16
24	8	17
25	9	17
26	9	18
27	9	19
28	10	19
29	10	20
30	11	20
31	11	21
32	11	22
33	11	22
34	12	23
35	13	23
36	13	24
37	13	25
38	14	25
39	14	26
40	15	26
41	16	26
42	16	27
43	17	27
44	17	28
45	17	29
46	17	30
47	18	30
48	18	31
49	19	31
50	19	32
60	24	37
70	28	43
80	33	48
90	37	54
100	42	59

*Exclude points on the median

For example, if there is a run chart with 25 data points and there are 20 runs, a quick glance through the preceding chart can tell us that there are some special causes present. These can be discovered by looking closely at the data and identifying any unusual event.

In addition to the preceding chart, the following rules can also point towards the presence of special causes:

Pattern	Plot	Analysis	Action	Example
Too few runs		Too few clusters of points above and below the median can indicate a cycle.	Find out what the clusters below the median have in common, and how they differ from the clusters above the median.	▪ Soups (Seasonal)
Too many runs		Too many clusters of points above and below the median indicate overcompensation, sampling from multiple sources, or data that may have been made up.	Find out what makes the high points different from the low points.	▪ Constant price changes
Shifts		8 or more points in a row on the same side of the median indicate a shift in a key element of the process.	Find out what was different about the process around the time that the shift occurred.	▪ Customer complaints increase due to change in policy.
Trends		7 or more points in a row continuously increasing or continuously decreasing indicate a trend.	Find out what was different about the process around the time that the trend started.	▪ Market growth or decline
Same Value		A sequence of 7 or more points having the same value.	Find out if measurement device is stuck. Poor resolution.	▪ Cycle time measured to nearest day.

As discussed earlier, standard statistical software such as Minitab and SPSS can help draw and interpret run charts very effectively.

A scatter diagram is another way to investigate whether there is any relationship between two variables, for example height and weight. One of these variables is plotted on the horizontal axis while the other variable is plotted on the vertical axis. The pattern of the points at which these two variables intersect provides an indication of the relationship between them. Please note that although a scatter diagram shows the relationship between two variables, it says nothing about the cause-and-effect relationship between them.

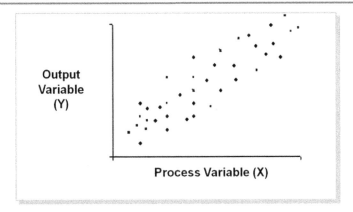

The type and strength of the relationship shown by a scatter diagram depends on a) the direction in which the data points are aligned, and b) how close the data points are to each other. Some examples are listed as follows:

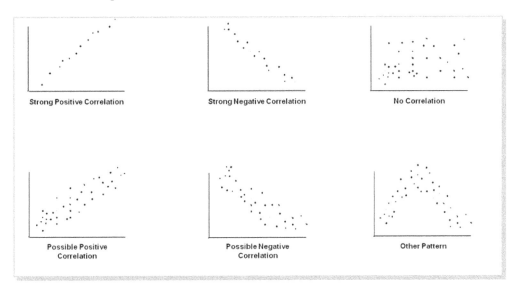

The **Pearson correlation coefficient,** denoted by **r,** can also provide a quantitative measurement of the strength of a relationship. This r value lies between -1 and 1. A value of -1 indicates perfect negative correlation, 0 indicates no correlation, and +1 indicates perfect positive correlation. Any value beyond 0.7 on either side of 0 indicates a fairly strong correlation.

An example of a scatter diagram and the correlation between two parameters of height and weight in a sample of students in a school is shown in the following screenshot:

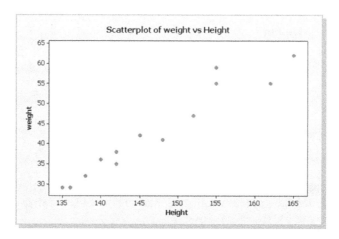

Here, weight seems to be increasing with height, but this does not imply that an increase in height causes an increase in weight and vice versa. Correlation does not imply causation. For example, a rooster's crowing at the break of dawn does not mean that it is the cause behind the sunrise.

The r value in the previous scatter diagram is 0.9, indicating a strong correlation between height and weight. This can be easily calculated using statistical software like Minitab.

Regression analysis is another statistical tool that can be used to study the relationship between variables. The best fitted line in a scatter diagram can approximate into a regression equation. In addition, it can also be used to predict values of the dependent Y using the values of dependent Xs. A simple linear regression looks as follows:

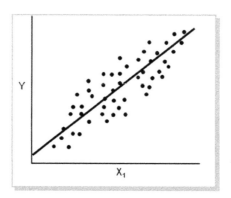

Where:

➤ Y = dependent variable or output

➤ a = constant or value of Y when X1=0

➤ b1 = slope of the line given by the ratio of change in Y per unit and change in X1

➤ X1 = independent variable

When there are multiple factors, the regression equation takes the form of
$Y = a + b1X1 + b2X2 + ... + bnXn.$

An example of such a regression that investigates infant birth weight in relation to factors such as gestational age and mother's age is as follows:

Infant birth weight	gestational age_weeks	Mother age
1.6	27	17
3.4	36	24
2.6	35	22
1.9	33	22
2.2	35	26
2.8	36	25
2.9	35	24
1.9	28	20
2.9	36	22
3.2	36	23
3.2	35	26
2.5	32	24
2.5	33	24
3.2	36	29
3.1	34	30
3.2	36	30
2.9	35	29
2.8	35	28
2.6	34	25
1.7	30	17

The regression equation is as follows:

Infant birth weight = - 2.73 + 0.130 gestational age, weeks + 0.0409 Mother age

Predictor   Coef SE Coef   T   P

Constant   -2.7345 0.8655 -3.16 0.006

gestational age, weeks 0.12980 0.03416 3.80 0.001

Mother age   0.04089 0.02418 1.69 0.109

S = 0.289088   R-Sq = 74.6%   R-Sq(adj) = 71.6%

The preceding output is a result of regression analysis through Minitab. As you can see, the infant birth weight can be predicted by the regression equation using the listed factors. The R-sq value indicates how well the model arrived at fits the data. It is a statistical measure of how close the data is to the fitted regression line. In other words, it is the percentage of response variable variation that is explained by the model. It can be represented as *R-squared = Explained variation / Total variation.*

The R-squared value lies between 0% and 100%. 0% indicates that the model explains none of the variability of the response data around its mean while 100% indicates that the model explains all the variability of the response data around the mean. Generally, an R-squared value of 50% or above indicates a good model.

In this example, it implies that 74.6% of the variability in the data is explained by this model. The higher the R-squared value is, the better the fit of the model to the data.

Another term that is important is p-value. For a relationship to be significant, this p-value should be less than or equal to 0.05 at a confidence level of 95%. We will discuss p-values later in the chapter.

This covers the various methods to analyze the data. Let's now look at the process to identify the value-adding and non-value-adding steps as well as delays in the process.

Process analysis (day 16-17)

We introduced the idea of a cross-functional diagram in the measure stage. This is a tool that has come from the Lean methodology. In the analyze stage, we examine each of the steps in the process from three perspectives:

➢ The nature of the work, namely value-adding (VA) and non-value-adding (NVA) steps

➢ The flow of the work, namely delays in the process

➢ Moments of truth

As discussed earlier, the value of a step is decided by its contribution towards the end product or service that the customer receives. If a step has a positive and transformative effect on the final end product or service, it can be classified as a value-adding step. Otherwise, it is a non-value-adding step. A non-value-adding step is anything you have to do again. Think of any word that is prefixed with "re":

➢ rework

➢ revise

➢ rejection

➢ repeat

➢ return

➢ recall

➢ redesign

➢ recheck

In Lean terminology, the ratio of the total time spent on value-adding steps to the total time taken by a process is called **process efficiency**.

The steps involved in a VA-NVA analysis are:

1. List all the steps in a column from the cross-functional diagram.
2. Write the time spent to complete each of these steps.

3. Brainstorm with the team to classify each of these steps as VA or NVA.
4. Calculate the percentage of time spent for each of these steps relative to the total time taken.

A hypothetical example of a process that has been analyzed for VA and NVA steps is given as follows:

Step	Time (hours)	VA	NVA
1	1	√	
2	5	√	
3	3		√
4	4		√
5	6	√	
6	2		√
7	1		√
8	3		√
9	1	√	
10	1		√
	27	13	14

The process efficiency of this process is 48%. This indicates that about 52% of the effort in this process is spent in performing non-value steps that have no impact at all on the final end product or the service. If we were able to reduce this, it will have a direct impact on cost and the turn-around time of the process. As part of improvement, the NVA are identified and minimized to improve the overall cycle time of the process. Also, it has been established that the higher the number of steps in a process, the greater the likelihood of defects being generated. Thus, the reduction of NVA steps has double the benefit – the reduction of defects and a reduction in the cycle time of the process.

Another aspect of process analysis is moment-of-truth analysis. A **moment of truth** is defined as any time when there is a likelihood of the customer making a critical judgment, positive or negative, about the service or their experience of your service. Moment of truth analysis involves identifying all the components in the process and ensuring that the customer has the best possible experience. A focus on moments of truth enables us to improve overall customer satisfaction and hence drive more business and revenue.

So far, we have been looking at the various ways of identifying the root causes of process issues; now, we will look at the possible ways to statistically validate these root causes.

Hypothesis testing (day 18-19)

In the previous sections, we analyzed the data to identify potential root causes. Since there is a lot of effort and capital at stake as part of the improvement project, it makes a lot of sense to *validate* and *confirm* these root causes. We need to ensure that the results that we observe are not due to *chance* alone. **Hypothesis testing** is one such way to do this. A hypothesis test calculates the **probability, p**, that an observed difference between two samples being compared can be explained by random or chance variation rather than any real, non-random, or significant difference between the underlying populations from which the samples have been picked up. If this p value is small, typically less than or equal to 0.05, we conclude that the samples are drawn from different populations, and hence the change due to improvement is real and significant.

This principle can be used to:

➤ Evaluate whether a proposed improvement is statistically significant or is due to random variation only

➤ Evaluate which of the several process factors have significant impact on the output

➤ Confirm the probability that the sample has been drawn from a population that follows a particular probability distribution, for example normal distribution

A hypothesis test is stated in the form of a **null hypothesis (H0)** and an **alternate hypothesis (H1)**. The null hypothesis states that the data belongs to one population and that any variation is due to chance only. On the other hand, an alternate hypothesis states that the data belongs to different populations. A lower value of p, less than or equal to 0.05, implies the rejection of a null hypothesis. Values greater than 0.05 would imply acceptance of a null hypothesis; there is no statistical difference in the data and any difference is due only to chance variations.

Make a note

A null hypothesis will be rejected for a p-value of less than 0.05.

There are numerous different hypothesis tests, and their application depends on a) the type of data, discrete or continuous, and b) the number of variables involved.

The following chart is a valuable guide to decide which test to use:

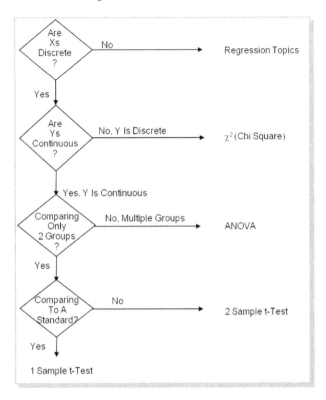

The following matrix diagram may also be used as a reference for various hypothesis tests that may be carried out depending on various X and Y combinations:

	Logistic Regression	Chi-sq Test Proportion Tests
	Linear Regression	Normal Y: T-Tests; Z Tests; ANOVA; ANOM, HOV (Chi-Sq Test, F-Test, Bartlett Test)
		Non-normal Y: Moods-Median Test, HOV (Levene's Test)

Discrete ... Continuous (Y axis)

Continuous ... X ... Discrete

Tip

Statistical software such as Minitab and SPSS can be used easily and effectively to conduct these tests.

As the matrix shows, some of these tests assume the normality of the data. So, before we proceed to use these tests, we need to ensure that the data that we have follows a normal distribution. We can use **normal probability plots** to objectively assess this. On a normal probability plot, data that follows normal distribution will appear linear. This test can be done using statistical software such as Minitab and SPSS. The following figure shows a normal probability plot created in Minitab. As you can see, the data is linear, and hence it follows a normal distribution. When data is found to be non-normal, you may like to consult a black-belt or master black-belt who can help you with transformations that can convert the non-normal data into normal data.

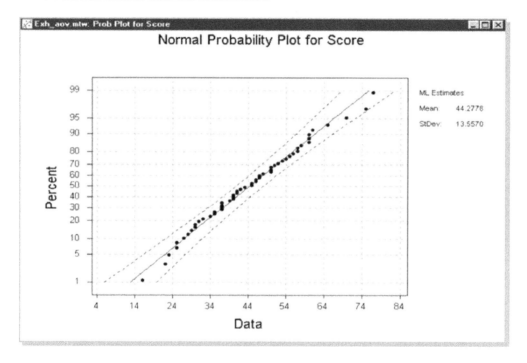

Another statistical concept called **homoscedasticity, or homogeneity of variance (HOV),** is important to bear in mind, especially when using tests like T-tests and ANOVA. This basically refers to the similarity of variance in the data sets being compared. If the variances between the samples being compared are large, the interpretation from these tests may not be accurate. There are various tests available to carry out HOV, such as Bartlett's test when data is normal and Levene's test when data is non-normal or samples are small. These tests are clubbed as Tests of equal variance in statistical software such as Minitab.

To sum up, before we run a hypothesis test, we need to check:

➤ The data type for X and Y

➤ If Y is continuous and X is discrete:

    ➤ Whether the data being used follows normal distribution

    ➤ Whether the data samples being compared have equal or homogeneous variances

For a detailed discussion on hypothesis testing, we recommend standard statistics texts such as:

➤ Statistical Inference by George Casella and Roger Berger

➤ Statistics by David Freeman, Robert Piasani, and Robert Purves

➤ Introductory Statistics by Neil Weiss

Hypothesis testing examples

A few examples can further elucidate the notion of hypothesis testing. We will be using p-values to decide whether a null hypothesis needs to be rejected or accepted.

The Problem:

A manager would like to know if the average time taken to resolve an issue is statistically different in two customer service centers (let's call them A and B) and how much this is to do with in-built processes or simply random occurrences.

The Solution:

We should first check whether the data follows a normal distribution using a normal probability plot. Once we ensure that the data is normal, we can proceed to the next steps.

Let's use the flow diagram introduced earlier:

➤ H0 = null hypothesis = AvgA = AvgB: There is no difference between centers

➤ H1 = alternate hypothesis = AvgA = AvgB: There is a difference between the two centers

➤ Y = average resolution time is continuous data

We are comparing two groups. Hence, the test to use is a two-sample t-test. Data for 30 points was taken for each of these units and Minitab was used to conduct a two-sample t-test.

The Minitab output is given as follows:

Make a note

Two-sample T for A vs B

	N	Mean	StDev	SE Mean
A	30	112.3	16.9	3.1
B	30	96.5	32.6	5.9

Difference = mu (A) - mu (B)

Estimate for difference: 15.77

95% CI for difference: (2.26, 29.27)

T-Test of difference = 0 (vs not =): T-Value = 2.35

P-Value = 0.023 DF = 43

As you can see, the p-value is less than 0.05 and the null hypothesis gets rejected. In other words, there is a significant difference between the two units, and these differences are not due to any random event.

The Problem:

A manager is interested in knowing whether there are significant differences between three teams working in shifts in the time taken to resolve queries.

The Solution:

As in the previous example, use a normal probability plot to verify whether the data is normal. Also, run a test of equal variance such as Bartlett's test to check HOV:

➤ Y = average resolution time is continuous data

➤ X = more than two groups

➤ H0 = There is no difference among the teams

➤ H1 = There is some difference

The test to be used is ANOVA. Data for 30 points for each of the teams, A, B, and C, was taken and ANOVA was used to analyze the data using Minitab. The Minitab output is as follows:

Make a note

One-way ANOVA: A, B, C

```
Source  DF    SS     MS      F      P
Factor   2  51130  25565  25.20  0.000
Error   87  88260   1014
Total   89 139391
```

S = 31.85 R-Sq = 36.68% R-Sq(adj) = 35.23%

```
                    Individual 95% CIs for Mean Based on
                    Pooled StDev
Level  N   Mean   StDev  --------+---------+---------+---------+-
A     30  112.30  16.86         (-----*-----)
B     30   96.53  32.56 (-----*-----)
C     30  153.10  41.22                         (-----*----)
                         --------+---------+---------+---------+-
                            100      120      140      160
```

Pooled StDev = 31.85

As you can see, the p-value is 0.00, which indicates that a null hypothesis stands rejected and that the three teams are statistically different from each other.

This section concludes the discussion on hypothesis testing. Now we have validated the root causes and we are ready to move to the next stage - **Improve.**

Case study – analyze

The team studied and analyzed the values of Ys collected during the measure stage. These distributions were analyzed for mean, mode, median, quartile values, and standard variation. The results and the targets for each of these are displayed as follows:

Measure	Actual Performance	Target
Customer satisfaction	3rd quartile = 70%	3rd quartile = 85%
Support cost per call	3rd quartile = $25	3rd quartile = $18
Days to final resolution	3rd quartile = 5.6 days	3rd quartile = less than 3 days
Wait time	3rd quartile = 6.4 minutes	3rd quartile = 2 minutes
Number of transfers	3rd quartile = 3.3	3rd quartile = 1

The various Xs impacting these Ys as collected as part of the data collection plan in the measure stage were analyzed using various tools like Pareto charts, multi-vari charts, fish-bone diagrams, tree diagrams, scatter diagrams, and so on. It was observed that the call types related to problems and version upgrades were the most expensive calls to the service. It was also observed that the three days of the week Friday to Sunday had the largest impact on the cost. Analyzing these further with the help of a fish-bone diagram, it was observed that staffing—the volume of calls ratio, number of call-backs, old FAQ documentation, the ratio of web-based and phone-based resolutions, and errors in the customer information database, including those that crept in the database while updating—contributed to these vital Xs.

Some of these critical Xs were also further analyzed using hypothesis testing tools such as a two-sample t-test and ANOVA. Finally, the team found out that inflexibility in staffing in relation to varying call volumes on different days of the week and the impact of call-backs on the wait time were statistically significant, with a p-value less than 0.05.

The team then revisited the project charter with respect to cost benefit analysis of the project and found that it did not require any major revision. The team was then ready to move to the improve stage.

This concludes the analyze stage, and we are all set to enter the next stage, improve.

Summary

The analyze and measure stages go together. The measure stage identified a large number of factors, or X's, that may have some impact on the output, Y. These are *potential* or likely factors for the output Y.

When we *analyze* these numerous potential factors, we observe that only a few of these have any significant impact on Y. The others are trivial factors in the sense that they have minimal impact on Y. In other words, the analyze stage can be referred to as the vital-few-trivial-many distinction stage.

There are a number of analysis tools that work with data, and there are other tools that analyze the process to reveal these vital few factors. These vital few factors can also be called root causes. Further validation and confirmation of these root causes is crucial as improvement projects involve investment of huge effort and resources. Hypothesis tests provide statistical validation for these root causes. The next stage, improve, then deals with actions to address these root causes. We will discuss the improve stage in the next chapter.

Quiz

1. Which of the following are the necessary prerequisites for an ANOVA test?

    a. Y is continuous, X is discrete

    b. Data is normal

    c. The samples do not display homogeneity of variance

    d. All of the above

    e. Only a and b

2. Two variables have a correlation coefficient of 0.75. Which of these statements is true in this regard?

    a. The slope of the line of the equation that represents the correlation is 0.75

    b. The variables are highly correlated

    c. One of the variables is the cause of the other variable

    d. Only a and b

    e. All of the above

3. An ANOVA analysis shows the following p-values. Given this data, which of these statements is true?

    a. A is the most significant factor

    b. B is the most significant factor

    c. C is the most significant factor

    d. None of the above

    e. All the factors are significant

4. Positive correlation implies that:

    a. The dependent variable improves as the independent variable increases

    b. The dependent variable decreases as the independent variable increases

    c. The independent variable decreases as the dependent variable increases

    d. The dependent variable increases as the independent variable increases

5. An R-squared value of 0.45 implies:

    a. For every unit increase in X, there is 45% increase in Y

    b. 45% of the time, the Y can be predicted correctly

    c. There are probably other variables that might be contributing to the variation in the response

    d. None of the above

    e. All of the above

6. The suggested hypothesis test when X is continuous and Y is discrete is:

    a. Linear Regression

    b. Chi-sq Test

    c. ANOVA

    d. F Test

    e. None of the above

7. Value stream analysis is used to:

    a. Find out VA and NVA activities

    b. Evaluate the flow of and the bottlenecks in the process

    c. Address moments of truth

    d. All of the above

    e. None of the above

8. Which of these statements is true with respect to p-values?

    a. At 95% confidence level, a p-value less than 0.05 indicates a statistically significant difference between the samples being compared

    b. For p-values less than 0.05, null hypothesis is rejected

    c. For p-values higher than 0.05, alternative hypothesis is accepted

    d. None of the above

    e. All of the above

9. The cycle time of a process is given by cycle time = 6.75*(number of documents processed) + 7.5. The correlation coefficient of this equation is 0.75. What is the predicted cycle time for 50 documents to be processed?

    a. 258.75

    b. 460

    c. 345

    d. Insufficient information

10. Which of the following can be classified as a non-value adding activity in a value stream analysis? A: Rework; B: Work in progress inventory; C: Personnel waiting for inputs; D: Product or process does not meet customer requirements:

    a. A

    b. All except A

    c. All except C

    d. B

    e. All of the above

Answers: 1 – e; 2 – d; 3 – b; 4 – d; 5 – c; 6 – e; 7 – d; 8 – e; 9 – c; 10 - e

>6

Improve (Days 20-25)

This chapter describes the fourth stage of the Lean Six Sigma implementation process, **Improve**. With the conclusion of the Analyze stage, we should have a clearer understanding of the root causes that contribute to the problem. The Improve stage takes the process forward by identifying actions that transform these root causes, resulting in an improvement in the effect—Y. This is where ideas and solutions are generated. These various ideas and solutions are then weighed against each other and the most effective solutions are implemented. This chapter will describe the deliverables of the Improve stage along with the tools and techniques to achieve them. At the end of the chapter, we will see the application of this stage to our case study.

Key deliverables

As we enter the Improve stage, we should have a clearer understanding of the areas where improvement is needed. We are now all set to generate, select, implement, and validate ideas. The key deliverables of the improve stage are:

➤ Generate ideas

➤ Select ideas

➤ Implement solutions

➤ Validate improvements

As usual, let's explore these deliverables in detail.

Generate ideas (days 20-21)

The first step in the improve stage is idea generation. We will explore some of the different tools and techniques for idea generation now.

Brain storming

Brain storming is used to generate numerous ideas on a topic in a relatively short period of time. The most commonly used technique involves participants simply calling out their ideas while the facilitator jots them down. There are other variations such as brain-writing where participants, instead of voicing their ideas, write their ideas on a piece of paper, which are then compiled by the facilitator. Sometimes the group may not be able to come up with ideas. For such occasions, we can use other variations such as analogy, in which a related subject is used to help the team generate ideas. For example, if the team is discussing ideas around how to foster team work, they may think of a baseball team and then generate ideas. Another technique is anti-solution, in which ideas for completely opposite objectives are discussed and then related to the current objective. For example, if the team is discussing ways to foster team work, an anti-solution would involve discussing ideas on how to destroy team work. From this position of negativity, the session can then move towards pointers for directing the team toward the real objective of fostering team work.

Some ground rules for effective brainstorming are:

➤ Do not dismiss any ideas or treat them as being stupid or wrong. Doing so might dissuade members from sharing further ideas.

➤ Team members should be encouraged to build on other ideas.

➤ Discourage the role of an expert in the session. This may lead to members getting into their shells and not contributing.

➤ The facilitator should be open-minded, able to capture ideas correctly and effectively, and able to communicate effectively.

➤ And most importantly—the session should be FUN!

Affinity diagram

This is often done in the post brain storming session. It involves generating ideas and then summarizing them logically into groupings based on "affinities," or relationships among the ideas. The objective is to develop meaningful ideas from a list of unrelated ones. Team members may write their ideas on Post-It notes and the facilitator then displays these notes. After going through the content of these notes, the team agrees on the various category labels. The team then places each of these notes under one of these categories. Duplicate entries are removed. Once the affinity diagram has been created, the team can then further discuss actions to address the various issues. An example of an affinity diagram is given as follows:

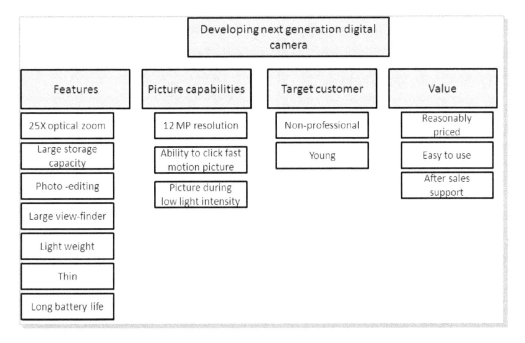

Force field analysis

Developed by Kurt Lewin, **force field analysis** is based on the principle that any change involves equilibrium between two opposing forces—the *driving force* and the *restraining force*. The *driving force* is the thing that helps to bring about change while the *restraining force* is that which acts as an obstacle to change. The team should write down the two "forces" on the opposite sides of a line (vertical or horizontal) and then debate which one of these has an advantage over the other.

The team also discusses and brainstorms the various ideas and ways to address these driving and restraining forces with respect to the project objective. The various ideas that are generated will then be prioritized based on some of the techniques outlined in the subsequent sections. An example is given as follows:

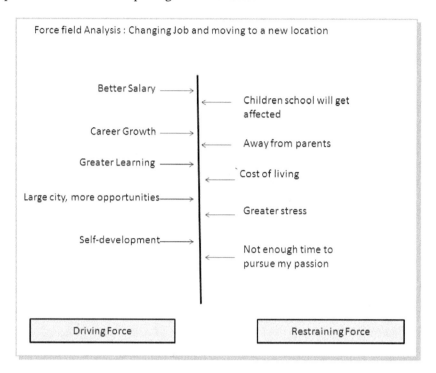

Force field Analysis : Changing Job and moving to a new location

Better Salary ———→   ←——— Children school will get affected

Career Growth ———→   ←——— Away from parents

Greater Learning ———→   ←——— Cost of living

Large city, more opportunities———→   ←——— Greater stress

Self-development———→   ←——— Not enough time to pursue my passion

Driving Force   Restraining Force

SCAMPER

SCAMPER is a mnemonic that stands for **Substitute, Combine, Adapt, Modify, Put to other uses, Eliminate**, and **Reverse**. This tool encourages the generation of new ideas for new products and services by assessing how to improve the existing ones. Questions about the existing products are asked using the seven prompts of the mnemonic. The following table gives sample questions for using SCAMPER:

Term	Sample Questions
Substitute	Can existing material or resources be substituted with other material / resources?
	Can an existing process be substituted with another process?
	Can the product or process be used somewhere else or as a substitute for something else?

Term	Sample Questions
Combine	Can the product / process be combined with some other product/process?
	What if the purpose and objectives are combined?
	Can the resource and talent be combined?
Adapt	How can the product / process be adapted or readjusted for some other purpose?
	Can an idea from some other process be adapted in the existing process?
Modify	How can the shape, size, and look of the product be modified?
	What else can be added to modify the product?
	Can some aspect of the product be highlighted to give rise to another product?
Put to other Uses	Can the product be used for something other than its intended use?
	Who else can the user be?
	Can the waste from the product / process be recycled to create something new?
Eliminate	Can some feature, part, or rule be eliminated from the product?
	Can the product be simplified?
	What can be understated?
	If a part is taken out, what will remain?
Reverse	What would happen if the sequence of the process / order in which parts are arranged in the product is reversed or modified?
	What roles could be swapped or reversed?
	Can the product / process be reorganized?

Select ideas (day 22)

We generated numerous ideas in the earlier section. Now, we need to select ideas that we will be actually working on. There are primarily two criteria to eliminate not-so-important ideas or solutions from the important ones:

➤ Eliminate those solutions with a low pay-off.

➤ Retain solutions that address "must" requirements. "Must" requirements are those requirements that must be met—they are obligations. These requirements can be important to the customer, related to law, government rules, and so on. These must requirements will have also been the result of the VOC exercise that we did in the Define phase.

An **effort-benefit matrix** is a tool to assess the pay-offs of the solutions. All the solutions are mapped into one of the 4 quarters of a 2 x 2 matrix of effort required to implement the solution and the benefit that the solution is expected to bring. An example is given as follows:

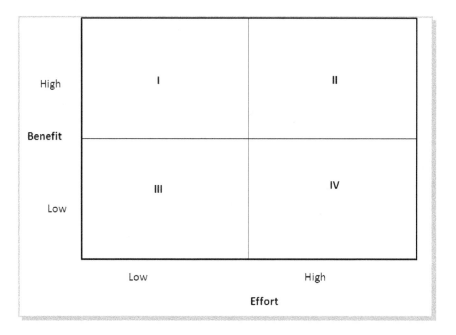

Solutions in quadrant I get the highest priority followed by quadrant II. Quadrant III and quadrant IV solutions can be eliminated.

The **nominal group technique (NGT)** is a technique that helps a team to reach a consensus on the relative importance of solutions by evaluating individual importance ratings to decide the team's final priorities. NGT works best with 6-8 solutions. The steps involved are:

1. Make a list of the solutions.
2. Each team member assigns a rank to each solution. The highest rank is given to the most important solution.
3. The rankings are then tallied and discussed for any potential surprises.

An example is given as follows:

From the preceding table, we find that solution B is the most important followed by E, F, and G. Also, wherever we find wide disparity in rankings, there can be discussion to understand the different perspectives.

We are now ready to implement the solutions that we have selected.

Implement solutions (days 22-24)

Our implementation plan involves the organization of project tasks and resources and the establishment of milestones, time lines, and actions to ensure that the project is successful. A good implementation plan has the following characteristics:

➤ A project definition with clear objectives

➤ A schedule with timelines and milestones

➤ Details of resources that the project will utilize

➤ Stakeholder analysis to ensure that there are no roadblocks

➤ A risk management plan to assess and mitigate risks

➤ Budget including costs involved

➤ Control in terms of data gathering and monitoring

Let's have a look at some of the well-known tools to implement and manage a project.

Work-breakdown structure (WBS)

This identifies all activities essential to carry out the project. As the name suggests, it breaks down the "work" at hand into manageable parts. Each WBS element is a discrete and separate activity with definite start and end points and measurable deliverables with a specific standard of performance. There are defined responsibilities for each of these elements. An example of a WBS for the construction of a building is given as follows:

WBS	Task
1	Scout the plot
1.1	Finalize the locality
1.2	Collect information on plots on sale
2	Evaluate finances
2.1	Evaluate the current finances available
2.2	Evaluate the loan eligibility
2.3	Evaluate various interest rates quoted by differnet banks
2.4	Finalize on the amount of loan
3	Registration of Plot
3.1	Agreement of sale with the seller
3.2	Registration of Plot with the local authorities
3.3	Final handover of plot from the seller
4	Construction
4.1	Approach various architects for designs
4.2	Evaluate designs
4.3	Evaluate builders
4.4	Finalize builder
4.5	Finalization of construction plan

Gantt chart

This is a type of bar chart that shows the project schedule. It gives the start and finish timelines for each of the project activities. An example is provided as follows:

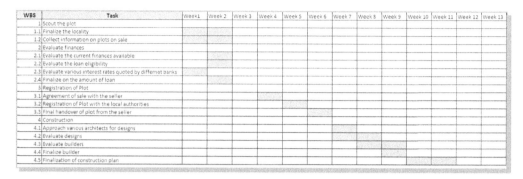

WBS	Task	Week1	Week 2	Week 3	Week 4	Week 5	Week 6	Week 7	Week 8	Week 9	Week 10	Week 11	Week 12	Week 13
1	Scout the plot													
1.1	Finalize the locality													
1.2	Collect information on plots on sale													
2	Evaluate finances													
2.1	Evaluate the current finances available													
2.2	Evaluate the loan eligibility													
2.3	Evaluate various interest rates quoted by differnet banks													
2.4	Finalize on the amount of loan													
3	Registration of Plot													
3.1	Agreement of sale with the seller													
3.2	Registration of Plot with the local authorities													
3.3	Final handover of plot from the seller													
4	Construction													
4.1	Approach various architects for designs													
4.2	Evaluate designs													
4.3	Evaluate builders													
4.4	Finalize builder													
4.5	Finalization of construction plan													

There are good project management tools such as MS Project available on the market that can facilitate the project planning and management exercise.

Risk assessment and mitigation

One of the critical aspects of project implementation is the risk assessment and mitigation plan. **Failure mode and effect analysis (FMEA)** is a well known tool for this. A typical FMEA looks like the one given as follows:

Process/Product: ———————
FMEA Team: ———————
Black Belt: ———————

FMEA Date: (Original) ———————
(Revised) ———————
Page: ——— of ———

			FMEA Process									Action Results				
Item/Proc ess Step	Potential Failure Mode	Potential Effect(s) Of Failure	Severity	Potential Cause(s) Of Failure	Occurrence	Current Controls	Detection	RPN	Recommended Action	Responsibility And Target Completion Date	Action Taken	Severity	Occurrence	Detection	RPN

An FMEA is a systematic and analytical quality planning tool that can be used at the production, design, process, and service stages to evaluate what can potentially go wrong and actions to mitigate the associated risks.

Potential failure modes are identified by the effect or consequences of these failure modes, the potential cause of these failures, and the current detection mechanisms. Each effect is assigned a **severity** rating on a scale of 1-10. The causes of the failures are assigned **occurrence** ratings on a scale of 1-10. The current detection mechanisms for these causes are assigned **detection** ratings on a scale of 1-10. The product of severity, occurrence, and detection ratings give a **risk priority number** (RPN).

Make a note

Risk Priority Number (RPN) = Severity (S) x Occurrence (O) x Detection (D)

The various RPNs can be used to select high priority failure modes, and the team discusses the steps that can be taken to mitigate these high priority failure modes. Once these actions have been implemented, RPN is recalculated to verify that the failure modes are now under control. The following diagram provides some rules of thumb on the severity, occurrence, and detection ratings:

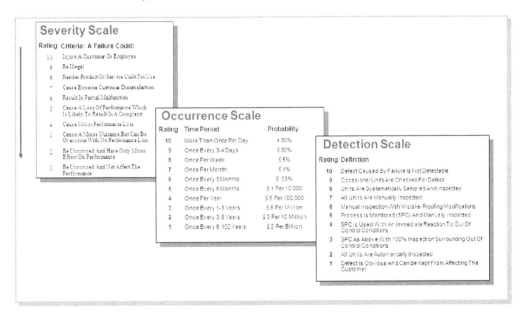

A working example of an FMEA is provided as follows:

Process/Product: Invoicing
FMEA Team: Invoice Process Mgnt. Team
Black Belt: E Jones
FMEA Date: (Original) 10/15/96
(Revised) 5/25/97
Page: 1 of 1

Item/Process Step	Potential Failure Mode	Potential Effect(s) Of Failure	Severity	Potential Cause(s) Of Failure	Occurrence	Current Controls	Detection	RPN	Recommended Action	Responsibility And Target Completion Date	Action Taken	Severity	Occurrence	Detection	RPN
Enter Amt Owed	Inaccurate	Overbill	8	Wrong Ct	8	Rare	9	57	DMAIC Team	E Jones	All DMAIC	8	4	2	64
				Wrong Price	5	"	9	6	to Investigate	5/15/97	Tasks	8	3	2	48
								36	Root Causes		Complete				
		Underbill	5	Wrong Ct	8	Rare	9	0	of Count &			5	1	2	10
				Wrong Price	5	"	9		Price			5	1	3	15
								36	Accessories						
	Missing	No Payment	6	Sale Error	5	Reviewed	3	0				6	5	3	90
				De Error	7	"	3	22				6	7	3	126
				De Error				5							
		Delay	3	Sale Error	5	Reviewed	3					3	5	3	45
				De Error	7	"	3	90				3	7	3	63
				De Error				12							
	Delayed	Late Bill	3	Sale Too Busy"	7	Measured	4	6				3	7	4	84
				System	3	"	4	45				3	3	4	36
				Down				63							
		No Bill	6			7	Measured	4				6	7	4	168
				Sales Busy	3	"	4	84				6	3	4	72
				System											
				Down				36							
								16							
								8							
			Total Risk Priority Number					2,204		Resulting Risk Priority Number					821

Some Lean manufacturing tools

Let's also look at some of the tools from Lean manufacturing that can also be used as part of the improve stage.

5 S

This forms part of Lean manufacturing and is used to improve the housekeeping of an operation. It is a structured and sequential method to improve workplace organization and standardization. "5 S" results in significant improvements to safety, efficiency, and productivity of processes, and helps foster a sense of ownership and pride in the employees. The five Japanese words that represent 5 S along with their English translations are given as follows:

> **Seiri (Sorting / Tidiness)**: Essential things are kept separate from non essential things.

> **Seiton (Set in Order /Orderliness)**: The objects and tools that are needed for the process are sorted and arranged in order and kept in clearly marked spaces. This helps with quick retrieval and optimal use of storage space.

> **Seiso (Shine /Cleanliness)**: The workstation and the surrounding areas are kept clean and tidy.

➤ **Seiketson (Standardization)**: Equipment is cleaned according to defined standards.

➤ **Shitsuke (Sustain / Discipline)**: The established procedure needs to be religiously followed. 5 S should be practiced daily and should become a way of life.

A schematic representation of the 5 S cycle is shown as follows:

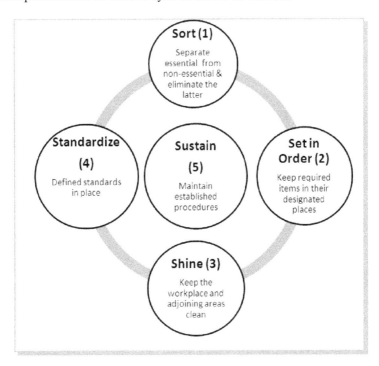

Although 5 S has its origin in the manufacturing world, it has found a wide acceptance in the service industry as well. It is a common misconception that 5 S as a workplace organization implies only housekeeping. This is quite myopic because workplace organization means much more than housekeeping and cleanliness. It refers to the way various components of a workplace system are defined, organized, and managed. These components may include things such as procedures, policies, rules, asset-ownership and management, inventory management, and so on. The strength of 5 S is its simplicity and the ease of adoption by every employee as it does not involve complicated tools and cumbersome data analysis.

Kaizen

Kaizen is the Japanese word for continuous improvement and deals with small incremental improvements in the processes.

The basic principles behind kaizen are:

➤ People are the most important asset of any organization

➤ The person closest to the process understands it the best

➤ Everyone can make improvements in their area

➤ Drastic improvements in and changes to a process are difficult to sustain over a period of time; gradual and incremental changes are more sustainable

It is based on the "3 M's" that have an adverse impact on the efficiency and productivity of any process. These 3 M's are Japanese words for the symptoms that call for improvements to be made in an organization:

➤ **Muri (Stress)**: Any task that leads to stress or requires a lot of strain to perform

➤ **Mura (inconsistency)**: Any task that results in inconsistent outputs

➤ **Muda (Waste)**: Any resource that is over-utilized or under-utilized

The kaizen process involves asking the 3 M's for each process. If the answer is yes for any of these, the teams should then discuss ways to mitigate or eliminate the problem. The standard **Plan-do-check-act**, also called the **PDCA cycle**, is used to implement the improvements and changes. This basically means one plans an improvement action, carries out the planned action, checks whether the action meets the desired objectives, and then takes the appropriate necessary correction as required. The entire cycle is repeated till the desired objectives are met.

Kaizen will always involve change in the method of doing a task. If an improvement does not involve a change, it is not kaizen. Typically, kaizen is not about data-led improvement and statistics, but is rather related to cultural and creative elements of a design, process, and so on.

Mistake proofing

Also called *poka-yoke*, this aims at preventing mistakes from occurring in the first place. The concept was developed by Shigeo Shingo and involves paying careful attention at each stage of the process and introducing appropriate checks at these stages. Mistake-proofing aims at the detection and correction of mistakes at the design stage itself so that defects are not generated during the production stage. The FMEA process can also introduce controls that act as mistake-proofing mechanisms. Some of the successful examples of mistake-proofing can be seen in the design of the SIM-card slot in a mobile phone, slots on audio and video cassettes that ensure that they can go inside the cassette player in one and only one way, and USB drives in computers.

Now we have begun to put solutions in place to improve specific processes, we need to validate these improvements—this will allow us to ensure that any changes we believe to be improving processes are doing exactly that!

Validate solutions (day 25)

So far, we have generated ideas, prioritized and selected the best ones, and then implemented them. We now need to validate the improvements after these ideas have been implemented. Validation primarily involves statistical validation of pre-and post-improvement data and the process. Hypothesis tests introduced in the analyze stage can be used for statistical validations. For improvements that are somewhat intangible, for example, that cannot be measured in terms of data, surveys for pre-and post-improvement conditions can be undertaken. For this, you need to return to the analyze stage; the analyze stage should be used continuously wherever you need to validate and check the results of any changes you are implementing. The process capability measure such as DPMO and Sigma level calculation post-implementation of improvement actions can be calculated and compared with that calculated during the measure phase. This comparison can quantify the achieved improvement level.

With this, we conclude the improve stage. We are now ready to enter the control stage in the next chapter.

Case study – improve

The root causes identified in the analyze stage were taken up by the team. The team brainstormed ideas to address these root causes. These ideas were then prioritized and selected using an Effort-Benefit matrix and NGT technique.

The actions included:

> ➤ Redesign of the staffing plan in line with the call volumes every day. Provisions were made to overstaff the Friday-Sunday period and under-staff on leaner days. An emergency back-up plan to address potential absenteeism was also created. The breaks on these days were also accordingly regulated to take care of spikes and troughs in call volumes.

> ➤ All the services that can be done through the web-based mechanism were revisited and incorporated accordingly. Communication plans were drawn to convince the customer how a web-based resolution would be as effective as a phone-based resolution. Certain incentives were also debated to encourage the customers to switch over to a web-based resolution.

> ➤ Various actions to reduce the number of transfers and callbacks were debated. The standard Frequently Asked Questions (FAQ) document was created. Some cross-skilling of customer service representatives was also planned.

All these improvement actions were then weighed on an effort-impact matrix. These actions were prioritized based on the effort taken and impact that these actions will have.

An implementation road map was created for these actions. The potential problem analysis and mitigation plans were also created using FMEA.

At the end of this implementation, the results were verified and validated using various hypothesis tests.

It was found that:

> ➤ Wait time reduced by 20 percent to about 5 minutes
>
> ➤ Volume / Staffing ratio reduced by 10 percent to 19.8 from 22
>
> ➤ Number of transfers reduced from 3.3 to 2.4
>
> ➤ Customer satisfaction also increased to about 76 percent
>
> ➤ Days to final resolution also improved by 12 percent to 4.9 days from 5.6 days

Thus, it was concluded that all the improvement actions implemented had a significant impact on the various measures. The team was now ready to move to the control stage so that these improvements could be sustained and institutionalized.

An FMEA study was also conducted to identify and plan actions to mitigate these risks. The pre-and post-improvement results were compared. The Sigma level before the improvement was 2.6-2.7 with a DPMO of 125440. The Sigma level after these improvement actions was 3.9 with a DPMO of 8300. Hypothesis tests were also carried out to validate that the improvements were statistically significant, and in all cases, the p-value was found to be less than 0.05, indicating statistically significant improvements. Now the team had to standardize the process so that these improvements were sustainable. This formed part of the control stage, which will be discussed in the next chapter.

Summary

The improve stage is really crucial as it is at this stage that the remedial actions to address the process are taken. The real transformative power of Lean Six Sigma should be felt at this stage. This is where creativity and innovation is most important; ideas are generated, discussed, and prioritized. Indeed, a broad consensus is essential for the improvements to be really effective, but discussion and debate are nevertheless healthy and useful in idea generation. Unlike the measure and analyze stages, the tools used in this stage are not statistical in nature but are broad, taking a holistic perspective of the involved systems and processes. This is crucial because if the solutions are not holistic, there may be serious negative side effects in other areas, which would ultimately reduce the effectiveness of the improvement. Quite often, because of the cost and effort involved, the solutions are first implemented as a pilot in a selected area under controlled conditions. Learning from the pilot solution is then extended to the larger area, which reduces the chances of other expensive errors happening.

After the improvements have been validated and realized, the next step is to create conditions to sustain these improvements. This is the subject of the next stage of the Lean Six Sigma implementation and is referred to as the control stage. The next chapter discusses the control stage. If the improve stage is about making things better, the control stage is about continuity – upholding your successes and keeping the good things going.

Quiz

During an FMEA, the RPN and associated severity, occurrence, and detection numbers were as follows for two failure modes:

1. Failure mode A : RPN = 450, S = 9, O = 5, D = 10, Failure mode B : RPN = 450, S = 5, O = 9, D = 10. Which of these two modes should get higher priority?

    a. A

    b. B

    c. Both A and B

    d. None of the above

2. Which of these statements is not true with respect to kaizen?

    a. Every employee can participate

    b. Addresses Muri, Mura, and Muda

    c. The person closest to the process knows most about the process

    d. A human asset is the least important asset of an organization

3. Which of these statements is not true with respect to 5 S?

    a. It is not applicable in an office kind of environment

    b. Discipline is extremely important to sustain the improvements resulting from 5 S

    c. Sorting refers to distinguishing between essential and non essential items

    d. Keeping things in their designated places may not be economical

    e. A and D

    f. Only A

4. While evaluating an RPN:

    a. The higher the number, the lower the risk

    b. The higher the number, the higher the risk

    c. Low detection ability increases the RPN

    d. High occurrence minimizes the risk

    e. B and C

5. In an assembly process, the process has been designed in such a manner that only correct components can fit in the assembly. This is an application of:

    a. Kaizen

    b. 5 S

    c. Value stream analysis

    d. Poka-Yoke

    e. None of the above

6. Which of the following is defined as continuous, incremental improvement?

    a. Just-in-Time

    b. Kanban

    c. 5 S

    d. Kaizen

    e. Poka-Yoke

7. During an FMEA exercise, the following values were observed for a failure mode: Severity = 6, Occurrence = 7, Detection = 5. What is the RPN?

    a. 21

    b. 210

    c. 2100

    d. 35

8. A Lean Six Sigma team has been assigned the task of improving an existing process. Which of the following tools should the team use to gain a clear understanding of the current process?

    a. Flow chart

    b. Process FMEA

    c. Pareto chart

    d. Design of experiments

9. A team has been asked to improve a process of resolving customer queries received through phone and emails. Which of the following tools should the team use to identify all the potential pitfalls and actual defects that can occur?

    a. FMEA

    b. Process map

    c. SIPOC

    d. Brainstorming

    e. SCAMPER

10. Rework, over-production, inventory, and motion are all examples of:

    a.   Waste

    b.   Special causes

    c.   Value-added activities

    d.   Kanban

    e.   Poka-yoke

Answers:

1 – A; 2 – D; 3 – E; 4 – E; 5 – D; 6 – D; 7 – B; 8 – A; 9 – A; 10 - A

>7

Control (Days 26-30)

This chapter describes the fifth and final stage of a Lean Six Sigma initiative, **Control**. This stage deals with the ways to sustain the improvements achieved in the previous stage. This is very crucial because without it, the improvements that have been made could be lost. For the organization to reap the benefits of the improvement, it is extremely important that these improvements are sustained and replicated throughout. This chapter describes the deliverables of the Control stage along with the tools and techniques to achieve them. At the end of the chapter, we will see the application of this stage to our case study.

Key Deliverables

The objective of the Control stage is to ensure that the improvements obtained in the previous stage are sustained and the lessons learnt are shared with the rest of the organization.

The key deliverables of the Control stage are:

➤ Process monitoring plan

➤ Control charts

➤ Project documentation

Let's look at these deliverables in detail.

Process-monitoring plan (days 26-29)

Without proper control mechanisms in place, a process can sometimes to slip back to its original state. **Process control** refers to a system of activities that helps to maintain the performance of the process in line with customer needs and drives the ongoing process improvement. It also helps to ensure uniform communication across process groups. A lack of uniform communication may lead to inconsistent outputs and rework efforts.

A **Process management chart** is a tool for process monitoring. The following diagram shows a process management chart:

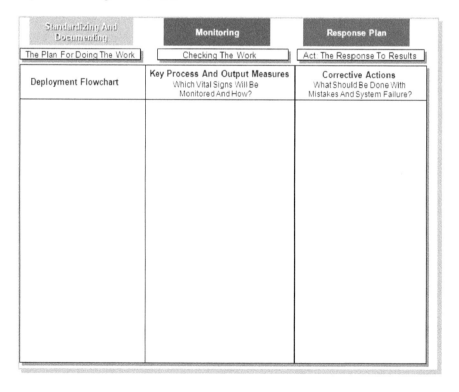

Standardizing And Documenting	Monitoring	Response Plan
The Plan For Doing The Work	Checking The Work	Act: The Response To Results
Deployment Flowchart	Key Process And Output Measures Which Vital Signs Will Be Monitored And How?	Corrective Actions What Should Be Done With Mistakes And System Failure?

It consists of three parts:

> ➤ **Standardizing and documenting**: As shown in the figure, this part deals with the plan for doing the work. Details of the steps of the process and who is responsible for these steps are provided in this section. The cross-functional process diagram discussed in the measure stage can be used here.

> ➤ **Monitoring**: This involves identifying key process and output measures for the process, standards, and targets for these measures, as well as a process to monitor to monitor these measures. We have discussed process and output measures in the measure stage.

> ➤ **Response plan**: This deals with identifying various responses that the team needs to take if the process does not operate as it was defined or if it is not meeting its specified targets.

An example is shown in the following diagram:

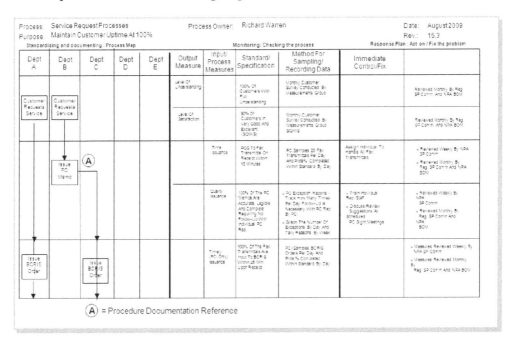

After process management chart, the process will now be monitored using control charts. The next section discusses control charts.

Control charts (days 27-29)

We first introduced control charts during the Measure stage. Control charts have a dual purpose:

> ➤ Similar to running charts, they can be used to analyze past data to determine past and current process performance

> ➤ They can also be used to assess whether the process is in control with respect to its specific standards.

While the Measure and Analyze stage utilize the first purpose, in the Control stage it is this second dimension that becomes important.

A typical control chart is shown in the following diagram:

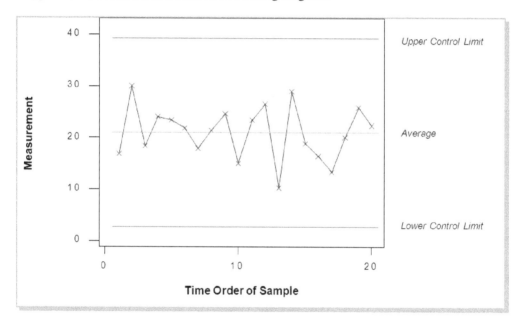

Control charts help to identify common and special causes of variation. This understanding is essential to control and improve processes.

There are two key characteristics of a control chart:

> ➤ The average or centerline that represents the central tendency about which plotted measures are expected to vary randomly.

> ➤ Control limits, both upper and lower, which represent the performance boundaries or limits expected for the process. Typically these are drawn on either side of the centerline at a distance of 3 σ.

It is important to remember that control limits and specification limits are different things; the following table summarizes the differences:

#	Control limit	Specification limit
1	It is defined based on the actual performance of the process i.e. +/- 3 σ from the mean	It is defined by the customer.
2	It is used to determine whether the process is stable and in statistical control	It is used to determine whether the process results in defects
3	It is plotted as part of control charts	It is usually plotted in histograms to observe defects
4	It changes when there is a change in the process	It changes when customers need change
5	Represents the voice of the process	Represents the voice of the customer

There are also different types of control charts. The use of these charts depends upon a number of different factors:

➤ Type of data, continuous or discrete

➤ Sample size

➤ Type of defect measure

The following flow chart provides information on when to use each type of chart:

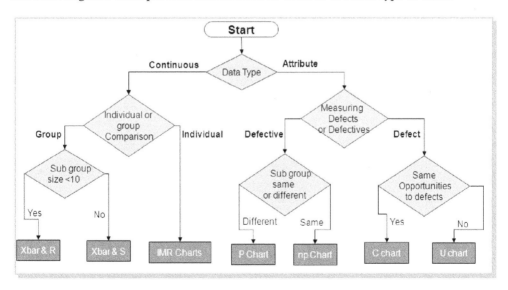

A process may have short-term as well as long-term variations. In order to capture both types of variations, the process is divided into sub-groups. A rational sub-group (also see *Chapter 4, Measure (Day 12-17)* is a sub-group of products that are created under conditions that are as identical as possible. For example, five consecutive products made on the same machine, the same setup, same raw materials and same operator would be a **rational sub group**. The variation in the measurement within this subgroup would be an indication of short-term variation. The variation in the measurement data between different subgroups would indicate long-term variation. The sub-group size may consist of 2-10 samples. Each of these sub-groups acts a snapshot of the process for a given point of time. Let's look at each of these different types of control charts in brief.

Control charts for continuous data

IMR Chart

IMR chart stands for **Individual and Moving Range** chart and it is used when one data point is collected at a point of time. The natural sub-group size is unknown. I-MR chart is actually two time-ordered charts that work in tandem. The top chart called **I** chart plots the individual data points with time and is used to detect trends, shifts, and patterns in the data. The bottom MR chart shows the short-term variations in the process. The moving range is actually the difference between two consecutive observations in the individual chart on the top. These two charts together thus monitor the average of and the variation in the process. As for the interpretation of these charts, typically, the R chart is analyzed first for any data points that fall out of control limits. This is then followed by a look at the I chart. The following diagram shows an example of I-MR chart for an insurance process and plots the cycle time taken to process individual claims. In this example, the MR chart at the bottom shows that all the data points fall within the control limits. The I chart at the top also shows that all the data points fall within the control limits. So, prima facie, the process seems to be in statistical control and is stable.

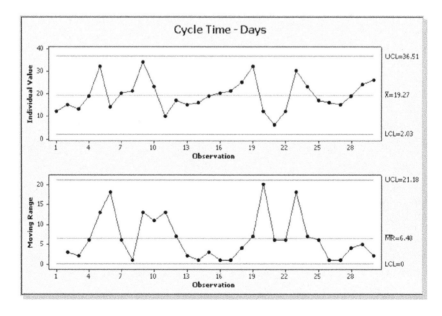

X-bar R chart:

Like the I-MR chart, this chart also consists of two charts working in tandem. Here, the measurements are collected in rational sub-groups of 2-10 samples. Each sub-group is a snapshot of the process at a given point of time. This is also a time-ordered chart. The top chart, also called the *X bar chart* plots the average of each sub-group and indicates the consistency of process averages. The bottom chart plots the range of these sub-groups and is a measure of the consistency of process variation. A typical X bar R chart for cycle time of resolution of customer queries with a sub-group size of 4 is shown in the following chart. Both the charts show that all the data points fall within the control limits. Hence, the process is in statistical control and is stable.

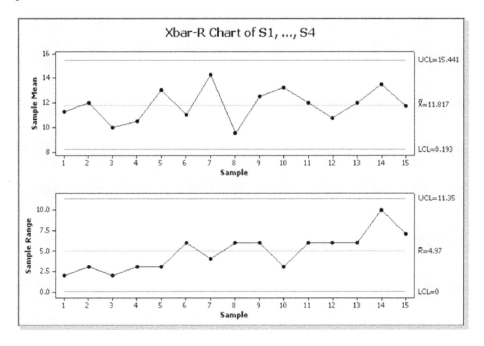

X bar S chart:

This is similar to X-bar R chart except that the subgroup size would be more than 10 and the bottom chart plots the standard deviation of each sub-group instead of the range in the X-bar R chart. The chart is analyzed and interpreted in similar manner to the X-bar R chart.

Control charts for discrete data

Before we begin discussing control charts for discrete data, let's briefly discuss the terms *defect* and *defective*. A defect, as discussed in *Chapter 4, Measure (Day 12-17)* refers to any instance when a customer requirement is not met. Defective on the other hand refers to a unit / product with one or many of these defects. Based on what we are measuring, the type of control chart used also varies.

C chart:

This chart is used when plotting defects in a sample. It assumes there is an equal sample size. The following example chart plots the number of incomplete fields observed in a sample of 200 applications received at an insurance provider's office. Since sample size is constant and we are plotting the incomplete fields or defects observed every day, we use the c chart. In the chart, we observe that all the values fall within the control limits. Hence, the process is in statistical control and is stable. However, since the chart also shows an increasing trend for the last eight data points, we need to observe the process closely to ensure that the process does not go out side the control limits in the immediate future.

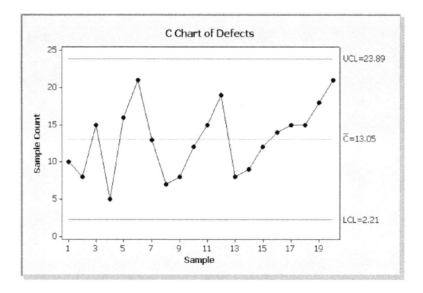

U chart:

This is similar to a c chart except that the sample sizes vary. However the defect per opportunity remains the same. The following example chart plots the number of incomplete fields in applications received everyday at an insurance office. However, the office receives a varying number of applications every day. As you can see, there are two data points that fall out side the control limits (shown here in red). Also, the last 7-8 data points show an ever increasing trend. We need to analyze these further to understand the underlying causes.

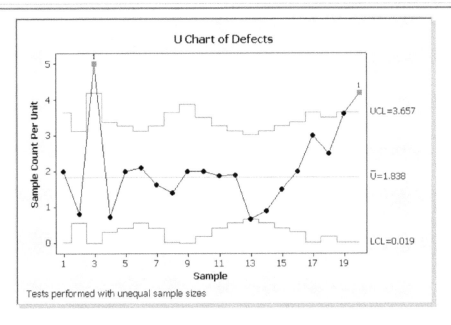

NP chart:

An NP chart is used when we have total count of defective units (units with one or more than one defects) with a constant sample size. The following NP chart shows the number of incomplete applications drawn from an equal sample size. As you can see, there are three instances when the data points fall out side the control limits. Thus, the process is unstable and is not in statistical control.

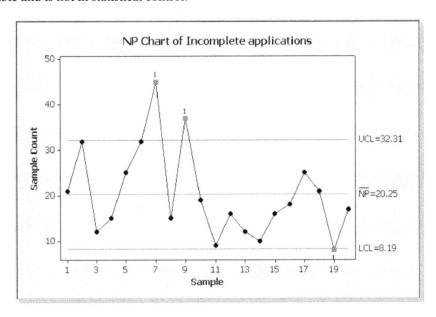

P chart:

The P chart is similar to the np chart and is used to monitor defectives with a difference that it deals with varying sample sizes. The following P chart plots a process of incomplete applications observed in different sample sizes.

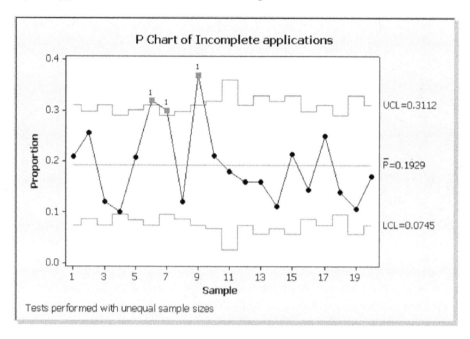

As you will have observed, the discrete charts do not use an extra chart to measure variation. The standard deviation for these charts are measured from the parameter (p, np, u, c) itself. Therefore there is no need for a range chart.

The control limits for these charts can be calculated using formulae provided in any standard statistics textbook. We have already provided references to some of these textbooks in earlier chapters.

However, standard statistical software such as Minitab and SPSS can be used to create the various control charts. These software use these formulae to plot the relevant control limits.

There are a number of warning signs that serve as a guide to identifying conditions that are out of control:

➤ One or more data points outside the upper or lower control limits

➤ At least two successive data points fall in the area beyond the line drawn at 2 σ from the center line in either direction

➤ At least four successive points fall outside the line drawn at 1 σ from the centerline in either direction

➤ At least eight successive data points fall on only one side of the centerline

If you ever encounter any of these conditions, the team needs to investigate whether any special cause can be attributed to them. If a special cause is identified, a root cause analysis followed by corrective actions must be taken.

This concludes the actual monitoring of the process. We now need to document the project that we were working on for final submission to the sponsor/champion.

Project documentation (day 30)

It is quite common to document the project in form of a storyboard. The following diagram shows one such storyboard. The storyboard provides a kind of narrative for the project in terms of the process followed for and results obtained from the various stages of DMAIC methodology. This helps to coherently bring out the approach used by the team as well as to share the knowledge the team gained in the process with others and for any future references. The storyboard should be clear, concise, and crisp and discuss key points. As you can see in the sample storyboard in the following diagram, each of the stages, corresponding deliverables and the results are displayed. The storyboard thus presents the narrative of the project improvement in a logical flow.

The project report should also be circulated to the finance and accounting division for review and validation of the financial savings. The project report with the financial validation and approval should be presented to the sponsor for formal approval and closure of the project.

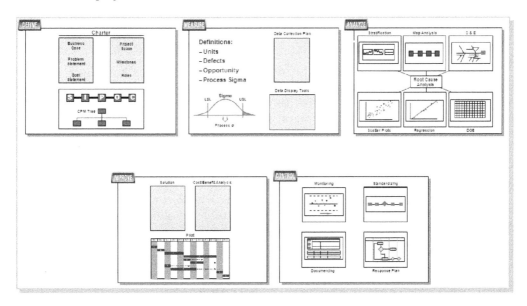

This concludes the control stage. This also concludes the DMAIC journey.

Case Study – Control

The Control stage of the case study will be discussed in this section.

The team created a process management chart. This chart consisted of the new and improved cross-functional diagram along with the metrics and ways to measure and report them. A response plan was also created that provided information on what to do if the process went out of control. A response plan was also created that provided information on what to do in case the process went out of control.

Various control charts were created and the relevant staff were trained on the usage and interpretation of these charts. They were encouraged to report any out of control situations to the concerned decision makers on time. This ensured that the defects were within control and could be detected easily.

The Ys and Xs from the improve stage were monitored for sustained improvement for 2 months, which provided 8 data points. All the data points showed an improving trend, leading the team to conclude that the improvements were sustained improvements. They then updated the control plans accordingly and rolled out the standard operating procedures and other standards to the entire team. The results were collected and it was found that the

a) customer satisfaction was found to be 86%
b) support cost per call had come down to $ 20
c) The days to resolution had come down to 2.7 days
d) Wait time had reduced to 2.4 minutes
e) number of transfers had reduced to 1.3.

The team had achieved its objective that was assigned by the champion. The team then presented the DMAIC storyboard to the process owner and the champion. They were delighted with the results that the team had achieved. The team was congratulated and was widely recognized in the organization based on their great success.

Summary

Achieving business excellence requires a lot of effort; it involves the difficult task of sustaining improvement and ensuring that this improvement is spread throughout the organization. Without this, the improvements would just slip back to the pre-improvement levels and all the efforts would go down the drain. The control stage addresses precisely that. The objective is to create mechanisms that help bring out wide scale awareness of the improved process.

Anything that is not tracked falls into disuse. Strong monitoring processes with defined metrics and targets help to keep improvements on track. But what do we do if the process goes off-track? A well-defined response plan ensures that the team is ready with effective responses to address any difficult situations.

As a logical conclusion to the end of the DMAIC project, the team prepares a project report that summarizes the efforts and results the team has achieved. This report is available for a wider audience in the organization so that the best practices and learning can be widely disseminated.

So, you have just concluded a basic Lean Six Sigma implementation in your organization. I am sure the journey will have been worthwhile. Hopefully, the DMAIC journey has been an exciting one and shows the kind of exponential transformation a structured problem-solving methodology with a sound foundation in statistical tools can achieve. Of course, every organization has had its fair share of challenges while implementing Lean Six Sigma, and doubtless you will have found it a challenging process, but these challenges force you to develop and create unique ways to handle them. The next chapter takes a close look at some of the best practices as well as pitfalls that an organization that intends to implement Lean Six Sigma can do well to pay heed to.

Quiz

1. A section within an automobile service center inspects cars post washing and cleaning. There are five parameters to be checked. Every day the total number of defects with respect to these parameters is plotted. The number of cars washed varies each day. Which control chart should be used?

   a. C chart
   b. I-MR chart
   c. P chart
   d. U chart

2. The control charts are used to:

   a. Check whether the process is performing as per the specification limits
   b. Check whether the process is stable
   c. Find out the cause of defects
   d. Identify the non-value adding activities

3. Which of these statements is true with respect to control limits?

   a. UCL and LCL are drawn at a distance of +/- 3 σ from the mean
   b. Control limits are same as specification limits
   c. Change in process does not impact the control limit
   d. All of the above

4. The control stage of a project includes:

   a. Process monitoring plan
   b. Standardization and documentation
   c. Communicating the lessons learned
   d. All of the above

5. Which of these statements is true with respect to a X-bar R chart?

   a. An X bar chart measures the average of the sub-groups

   b. A R chart measures the range between the sub-groups

   c. It is independent of when and where the samples are picked up from in the process

   d. The two charts measure one and the same thing, though in a different way

6. Which of these statements is true with respect to a U chart?

   a. It is used for defective with a constant sample size

   b. It is used for defects with a constant sample size

   c. It is used with defects with a varying sample size

   d. It is used with defective samples with a varying sample size

7. Which of these statements is true with respect to interpretations of a control chart?

   a. Points outside control limits indicate a process that is not in statistical control

   b. At least two successive data points fall in the area beyond the line drawn at 2 σ from the center line in either direction

   c. At least four successive points fall outside the line drawn at 1 σ from the centerline in either direction

   d. At least eight successive data points fall on only one side of the centerline

   e. All of the above

8. Documented procedures as part of process control:

   a. Must have provisions for human error

   b. Standardize the process

   c. Divert resources where required

   d. All of the above

Answers:

1 - D; 2 - B; 3 - A; 4 - D; 5 - A; 6 - C; 7 - E; 8 - D

>8

Best Practices and Pitfalls

A Lean Six Sigma implementation, like any organization-wide initiative, has its own challenges and pitfalls. Over the period, many organizations have implemented Lean Six Sigma, and they have had their own fair share of these challenges and unique ways to overcome them. This chapter discusses some of the best practices and challenges that these organizations have followed and faced in the course of the implementation. This will help us steer away from the potential pitfalls and leverage the learning and the best practices.

Best practices

Let's look at some of the best practices first.

The power of stretch goals

Lean Six Sigma is an exponential improvement methodology that results in breakthrough improvements. To help realize its transformative power, the improvement goal should be a stretch goal. Typically, a stretch goal would imply at least 50 percent improvement over the current performance. An example could be if the current productivity level is 15 units / day, the improvement goal should be at least 23 units/day (about a 50 percent improvement).

Benchmarking against the competition can be another very powerful way to set a proper stretch target. Benchmarking refers to the process of comparing the existing process and performance metrics with that of the best in the industry or the best practices from other industries.

Ready-aim-fire

It is a common observation that people tend to jump to conclusions without proper planning. This is, to a great extent, because of what psychologists refer to as action bias, which refers to the tendency of relating effectiveness to activity. An action is always preferred over inaction even if the latter is more sensible in a given context. Lean six sigma, as a methodology, believes in a structured way of solving the problem. This involves a well thought out plan, a data-driven analysis for root causes, and then a "measured" improvement plan. It would do great wonders for any organization to create a culture where reflection is given due weightage over mindless action. *Ready, aim, and then fire instead of ready, fire, and aim.*

In God we trust, all others must bring data

Data improves the quality of decisions dramatically. It helps to identify and select ideas and solutions that are truly the best and most effective ones. All world-class organizations encourage a culture of data-driven decision-making processes. A successful lean Six Sigma initiative will truly thrive and reach its full potential in such a culture. A very popular six sigma slogan goes like this: "*In God we trust, all others must bring data.*"

Tangible targets linked to financial measures

Each Lean Six Sigma project must be linked to tangible financial measures such as money saved, new revenue generated, costs avoided, and so on. There should be well-defined mechanisms to measure, track, and roll up these financial measures. Tangible targets help to keep the team focused and energized, and it has often been observed that the teams achieve much beyond the targets that the team set out at the beginning of the project.

Variation is the voice of the process

Genichii Taguchi, the management guru from Japan and the father of design of experiments, expressed quality as a loss function. According to this principle, the quantum of loss perceived by the customer is proportional to the square of the difference between the target and the actual values. In other words, the performance begins to gradually deteriorate as the design parameter deviates from the optimum value. Taguchi's loss function can be represented by the following equation:

$Y = K(X-T)^2$

Where:

- ➤ Y = Loss
- ➤ K = Constant
- ➤ X = Actual measured value
- ➤ T = Target value

This equation can be graphically represented as:

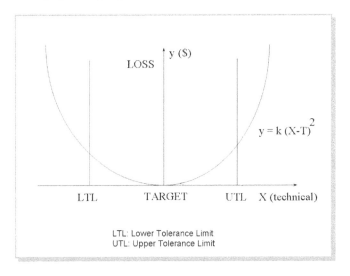

LTL: Lower Tolerance Limit
UTL: Upper Tolerance Limit

For example, having a high average of the number of orders is a good thing. However, imagine a situation where there is a huge variation in the number of orders received daily. This will lead to chaos; it would be a nightmare in terms of capacity and resource utilization – machines will either run at full capacity or sit idle, and resources would work overtime or simply have nothing to do.

Lean Six Sigma helps to narrow down the range of variation in any process, product, and service. It also helps make the process robust enough to absorb any variation due to conditions that are not within the control of the team.

Celebrate achievements

This is very important. Celebrating achievements regularly irrespective of the quantum of success keeps the team motivated and helps sustain the initiative for a longer run.

Involve the owner of the process

Among the top three reasons why the deployment of Lean Six Sigma fails is because the owners of a process who have the maximum stake in its improvement have not been taken along throughout the entire improvement process. It is absolutely crucial that the Lean Six Sigma team regularly communicates and involves the owner during the entire journey of the project.

Project goals should be aligned to organizational goals

This sounds clichéd, but during implementation, this is often the most overlooked aspect. The selected projects should be prioritized strictly on the basis of their alignment with the organization's business objectives. Otherwise, it is very likely that the initiative will derail very soon.

Pitfalls

Now let's look at some of the pitfalls.

"Our process is so different"

This is one of the most common myths and refrains that people express, especially during the early period of Lean Six Sigma deployment. It is quite natural to consider my area so unique that whatever has worked for others or in other areas would not work in mine. It is important to realize that Lean Six Sigma is *process or area agnostic*. It has proven itself time and again in diverse areas, and there is hardly any field where it has not been successfully applied. Steer clear of this misconception that you are an exception to the rule—Lean Six Sigma can certainly work for you if you let it.

Relying blindly on data

In the earlier section, we discussed how critical it is for organizations to have a data-driven environment. However, it is equally important to ensure that the systems and processes that churn out the data for decision-making are regularly validated. Using a measurement system that generates incorrect data may prove to be an expensive mistake.

Projects with too large a scope

One of the prime reasons for the failure of Lean Six Sigma projects is inadequate scoping. Very often, the scope chosen becomes unwieldy for the team, and they are not able to focus properly. It is always advisable to have a smaller scope than a large scope that has a high risk of failing. Target the project and keep it specific.

Needless use of statistics and tools

Often, Black Belts can tend to use statistical tools just for the sake of using them because their training and textbooks have advised them to do so. This results in unnecessary loss of time and effort. We need to remember that these tools are our servants, and we should use them as we like instead of becoming their servants. Use tools judiciously and where needed, because otherwise, it can just be an overkill without any value addition.

Part-time Black Belts

Organizations that look for breakthrough results using Lean Six Sigma need to realize that they need a set of people who will dedicate all their time to drive projects that are aligned to business objectives. Assuming that the organization will be able to reap breakthrough improvements by having part-time black belts who have other responsibilities in addition to lean Six Sigma projects is foolhardy. This approach will simply not be able to generate the focus and the force necessary to sustain the change that the organization intends to bring with lean Six Sigma deployment. Projects tend to drag, savings get adversely impacted, team motivation and morale become thin, and the credibility of the initiative gets a dent.

Over training

A lot of organizations unnecessarily spend a lot of effort and money on Lean Six Sigma training more than is required. Every employee need not be a Black belt. A good rule of thumb when deriving the percentage of people relative to an organization's strength was discussed in the second chapter under the section *Enable*.

Inflated opportunity counts

As we discussed in *Chapter 4, Measure (Day 12-17)*, defects per million opportunities or DPMO is a widely used method to calculate process performance capability. Sometimes, in order to show a process in a better light, practitioners can falsely inflate the number of opportunities to make the denominator in DPMO large so that the overall DPMO goes down and the sigma level looks healthier. The thumb rule is that opportunities should always be from the perspective of the client. After all, if you have a lower DPMO because of an inflated opportunity count, you're only deceiving yourself!

Inadequate use of automation or technology

Leveraging technology and automation only helps the Lean Six Sigma initiative hugely. The quality and efficiency of the initiative moves up multiple notches when technology is applied in the right manner. It can be leveraged in all aspects of the initiative, right from skill enhancement to the process of project registration to project tracking and approval.

Keep these elemental do's and don'ts in mind while designing your Lean Six Sigma program; this will certainly make it effective and easy to handle.

Summary

This concludes our book! We hope you enjoyed the Lean Six Sigma implementation journey as much as we did sharing our experience with you. We wish you all the best for your Lean Six Sigma implementation.

www.ingramcontent.com/pod-product-compliance
Lightning Source LLC
LaVergne TN
LVHW081346050326
832903LV00024B/1337